# CONCILIUM

*Religion in the Seventies*

# CONCILIUM

*Concilium*, December 1977: Moral Theology

# MORAL FORMATION AND CHRISTIANITY

Edited by
Franz Böckle and
Jacques-Marie Pohier

A CROSSROAD BOOK
The Seabury Press • New York

1978
The Seabury Press
815 Second Avenue
New York, N.Y. 10017

Library of Congress Catalog Card Number: 78-55543
ISBN: 0-8164-0368-6
ISBN: 0-8164-2169-2 (pbk.)
Printed in the United States of America

241.

# CONTENTS

## Part III
## The Situation of the Ecclesial Society in
## Moral Formation

# Editorial

WHAT is the point of examining Christian moral formation in a *Concilium* devoted to moral theology, above all when 'moral education' or 'moral training' is not concerned primarily with a theory of moral conscience and the moral standards that ought to define it, but instead with the larger and more diffuse process by which a society and a civilization more or less voluntarily imbue people with values of which they themselves are not always conscious?

A subject like this might seem to have much more to do with practical theology, or even sociology of religion. It does indeed, but we thought that it should also be studied from the specific viewpoint of moral theology.

In fact the role of Christianity in moral training has been considerably modified since the middle of the nineteenth century in most Christian countries of Europe and northern America. It will certainly undergo similarly radical change, though of a different kind, in Latin America and the Catholic communities of Africa and Asia. For the greater part of its history the Catholic Church was charged with the main responsibility for the moral training of individuals and groups, when it operated in deep symbiosis (which does not exclude conflict) with other bodies concerned with moral education (families, states, and so on).

For more than a century, however, the ecclesial community has no longer been the main source of moral training, and the values to which it wished to educate its charges are far from being shared, or often even tolerated, by other bodies concerned with moral formation. There are other morals and other values. Even when the Church acknowledges the legitimacy of such instances and entities, or of their values, that evokes a new situation with consequences and bases which are properly theological in nature. J. Neumann considers this complex of problems. The difficulties and possibilities of the transition from the former to this new situation are effectively illustrated by what

M. Benzo has to say about the state of things in Spain between 1939 and 1975.

Another change in the field under consideration relates to the fact that the development of the social and psychological sciences has allowed the discovery of some of the psychological and social mechanisms which determine moral formation (and the formation of the intellect, socialization, and so forth). This knowledge of the mechanisms of moral education has given a certain 'power' to the theoreticians and practitioners of these sciences. The Church, already in difficulties when trying to co-operate and reach agreement with other social agencies of moral training, is faced now with a different type of competence and power. K. Ryan's article shows that this process is not untroubled, and that Christian entities concerned with moral education—like other such bodies—can be completely powerless when faced with this new knowledge and power. The example is all the more striking when we remember the leading position in moral formation of the various religious denominations in the United States, where differences between denominations are often seen almost exclusively in terms of differences in morals and moral training.

But the most important change in the situation of Christianity in regard to moral formation is undoubtedly that resulting from a development within Catholicism itself, whose ground is specifically theological. We are all aware of the discussions of more than thirty years on what theologians have called 'the specifically Christian'. N. J. Rigali states in this issue that the outcome of the debate is on the whole inadequate, and asks whether the question was posed appropriately. These discussions have important consequences for moral training. If there are no forms of moral behaviour which are specifically Christian in their material aspect, Christian moral training cannot be *specifically* concerned with education for certain forms of behaviour in their material aspect. In fact a number of other moral systems require or forbid forms of behaviour which Christianity requires or forbids. Obviously, for example, in regard to such problems as abortion or divorce Catholics have not been the sole defenders of certain positions. If moral education means making an individual and a social group capable of eliciting certain values and of advancing the cause of the 'good' (in the profound ethical sense of the word), then where are we to look for the specific content of Christian moral training? Far from being uniquely an educational or practical problem, the question is rightly a fundamental problem of moral theology.

Since we are unable to locate it in the specific nature of the forms of behaviour to which it is supposed to educate its charges, it seems permissible to set the specificity of Christian moral training in, for instance, the three great theological virtues on which, since the beginning of Christianity, the essential content of Christian morality has been more or less systematically centred. We have not followed that course; but the reason was not of course a wish to deny the radical primacy of the theological virtues. It was because we thought that Christians could not claim a monopoly of faith, hope or charity. To keep to the religions descended from a common monotheism, surely faith and hope are less important in Judaism and Islam than in Christianity. Surely it is right to say that loving God with his own love and loving one's neighbour with the love God has for him is less a grand inspiration to the great Jewish and Muslim men of faith than to the great Christians.

We therefore had to ask if the unique aspects of the Christian God have endowed Christian moral training with original features. That was appropriate in moral theology on the one hand, and in moral formation on the other hand. 'Finis operantis est fons moralitatis', in fact. It is permissible to formulate the primacy of charity and the way in which, in a scholastic sense, it 'informs' the whole Christian endeavour by saying that in charity God becomes for the believer the 'finis operantis' of all that he does. That does not of course exclude the possibility that the believer might ordain for himself other objectives and even ends than God, for (if we follow Thomas Aquinas in this) charity has several objects: God is the reason for loving, but is the unique object of love. If we have to mark out a specific content in Christian morals, it is in the way in which God attends the banquet of our moral life and becomes for us a reason to love all things and all beings, beginning with him, and in which he makes himself a reason for our living and acting.

The specific content of Christian morality would then be the way in which God is *ratio agendi, ratio diligendi* in that process: the reason to act and reason to love. If the Christian God has something specific about him, then that specific something would be the way in which God is Christians' reason for acting and loving. It is good theological methodology to look at what is specific to the Christian God in order to find what is specific to Christian moral training.

But it is also good methodology because it *is* a question of training—of formation. To train or to form is primarily to imbue with desire, to inspire and to motivate. It is not that alone but it is that first of all: from the most elementary identification processes at the most mysterious sources of personalities and groups, to the most sensitive and noble forms of the realization and imparting of values. Since we are concerned with Christian moral training, we must show how God who revealed himself as the Father and in Jesus Christ, and whose Spirit inspires us in the Church, imbues us with desire, and inspires and motivates Christian behaviour. Christian moral education consists primarily in imbuing people with a desire to act in a certain way because God is what he is; with a desire to live thus because God showed himself living thus.

That is why a major section of this *Concilium,* the first part in fact, shows how the uniqueness of the Christian God is an original reason for living, acting and loving: that God is the Father, as he showed us in Jesus Christ (A. Vergote); that Jesus Christ was what he made himself and what God made him (N. J. Rigali); and that God is a Spirit who gives life (P.-T. Camelot). An Old Testament specialist (R. Murphy) shows us what was original in the way in which the God of Abraham, Moses, David, Isaiah and Ezekiel wished to found a nation and how that is a unique and fundamental aspect of the Christian endeavour.

But, however original the way in which the Christian God inspires action and becomes a *finis operantis* of any Christian act, Christianity still does not have the monopoly of moral training. Others make it an object of thought and action. It is fortunate that Polish theologian, H. Juros (we too rarely hear from Polish Christians) has been able to offer a methodological study of conscience formation, which he says is not a specifically Christian task. Yet this individual and collective formation of conscience encounters a number of obstacles which Christian moral formation, no less than any other, also has to face. Should we educate for freedom or obedience (A. Auer)? Which must we promote more: the blossoming of the individual or the collective formation of the world (H. de Lavalette)? Should we develop ethical codes by 'preaching on the mountain', or revivify life by overthrowing social barriers and 'dining with whores' (J. Pohier)? As H. de Lavalette remarks, it is often a question of false dilemmas in such cases, and it is necessary (as J. Pohier says, and that is good logic) to admit a third term which resolves and dissolves what is false in the excessive polarization of the dilemma. Of course, in practice moral training shows that it is not always so easy to make this kind of choice successfully. Here too we must see if Christianity has anything original to say.

We have reached our real goal if we have contributed a little to what should be the essence of Christian moral formation: imbuing with a desire to live, act and love in a certain way because we discover in the Church that God, Father, Son and Holy Spirit, lives in a certain way; and because we find that gives us a desire to share his life and to make it shared as he wishes us to make it shared.

FRANZ BÖCKLE
JACQUES POHIER

# PART I

*In What Way Is the Christian God a Specific Reason for Action?*

# Antoine Vergote

# God Our Father

THE consequences of the close relationship between faith and practice are paradoxical for those, whether Christians or not, who expect a specifically Christian morality. One often notes, in fact, that the actual formulation of rules which are held to be specifically Christian expresses contingent convictions decided by a certain historical context. Moreover, in essence, Christian principles are to all intents and purposes universal, and the Church adopts moral directives due to the efforts of thoroughgoing secular humanists. This ambiguous and sometimes baffling nature of Christian morality relates, I am convinced, to the Christian unity between faith and practical morality, both of which have the divine Fatherhood as their one ground.

Jesus' affirmation of the divine Fatherhood was not an entirely new idea of God. However, the unique aspect of Christ's message consists in his wholly original presentation of that divine Fatherhood. Accustomed as we are to derive any message from general ideas conceivable in theoretical terms, we tend to render Christ's message insipid and to explain the divine Fatherhood in terms of such general qualities as kindness, patience, all-powerful creator, law-making authority, judge, and so on. To be sure, these terms adequately designate the various relations of the Father to his children. But if we limit ourselves to a description in this way of the content of the notion of fatherhood, all we do is to repeat the general religious idea of a divine Fatherhood. Then it does not ground a moral philosophy. The originality of Jesus' message is that it does not offer an *idea* of God's Fatherhood, but its practical expression.

3

We know that Jesus addressed his God in a very personal way which was totally new and unusually intimate: *Abba*. This totally confident familiarity, allied with respect, does not express a purified and deep religious feeling but awareness of messianic election and destiny. The expression 'my Father' accords with a declaration and an initiative from God who effectively makes himself Father for Jesus and, through him, for mankind. For and through Jesus, the divine Fatherhood is not a general idea—a metaphor, as Kant thought and, following him, a large number of Christians who are more heirs of the Enlightenment than of Jesus Christ. God's Fatherhood is an event, a mystery in the original sense of the word: the affective advent for man of God as Father. Christian morality, like the practice of the faith, depends on this event.

Before considering the consequences of this principle of faith and behaviour, I should like to throw some light on the meaning and the frame of reference of Christ's unique message by examining the notion of human fatherhood. There is a startling analogy. Far from suggesting that this representation of the Father-God is only symbolic in the sense of a general religious idea, formed by the projection onto God of human experience, this analogy shows that divine Fatherhood is authentically practised only in the historical action in which God made himself Father. That which, in the human order, is specific to father (in comparison with, that is, the maternal figure) is that the father shows himself as father in exercising his own unique qualities in his personal relationship with the child. The mother is naturally present to the child through the spontaneous symbiosis of bio-affective bonds. Everything she stands for in the sense of specifically maternal values reproduces these qualities of intimacy, inwardness, welcome and tenderness. The father, in order effectively to be the father, must assume the function of paternity in acknowledging his child. It is worth remarking that among a number of peoples adoption is a lesser form of fatherhood, for it is in the nature of the father, even the biological father, to adopt the child as his own. The text of Psalm 2:7 (which is cited several times in the New Testament and invoked in the liturgy) also expresses the truth that God made himself the Father of Jesus of Nazareth by investing him, by a specific initiative, with the rights, dignity and mission of the Son: 'You are my Son. This day I have begotten you'. It is because it is the father's function to institute the paternal relationship and to invest the son with the bond of sonhood that the paternal function has an ethical dimension, as we shall see.

The ambiguous status of Christian morality is clear when we see it as the behavioural practice of faith as consent to the manifest initiative of divine fatherhood. On the one hand, God, as the Creator, the all-

powerful Father who has made the heavens and the earth, is the ultimate ground of the morality of any religious man. Even if an unbeliever
takes the word 'God' only as a symbol of what he understands as the
sacred aspect of human life, he will agree with the religious man in
extolling ethical values which are universal because they are essential
for man's very humanity: justice, thou-shalt-not-kill, respect for truth,
and so on. In affirming faith in the Creator as the first point of the creed,
Christianity necessarily accepts the universal rules of morality. Hence
in essential content, Christian morality is philosophical in nature, for it
is established on the principles of reason. But the attachment of faith to
the advent of the fatherhood of God and to adoptive sonhood bring with
it consequences in the life of faith which are specific to that life. Can
these still be termed moral? The answer is not so easy. In my opinion,
they have a moral field of reference because they bear upon moral
behaviour. To refer to a traditional distinction, we would say that they
transform existence and that consequently they provide the spiritual
energy to promote what is in essence universally moral. Christian faith
in God the Father is not the theoretical affirmation of a truth pronounced by a religious man. It is the active acceptance of a proffered
relationship. 'I believe' is a *performative* expression. In it I implicate
myself, and commit myself to a lived relationship which transforms my
existence, in the same way as and more basically than the man and
woman who, when they marry, establish a relationship and commit
themselves to live in accordance with the terms of that establishment.
Hence a believer's life is an ethical radiation-point within mankind.

### THE MEANING OF DIVINE FATHERHOOD AND ITS
### PRACTICAL CONSEQUENCES

## Fatherhood and Law

Jesus undermined 'the Law', a basic Jewish point of reference and
cultic object. That was the main reason for the enmity of the scribes
and pharisees and the cause of his death sentence. But, far from sup-
pressing the Law, Jesus took it back to its source: the will of God. The
whole law depends on the first and greatest of the commandments. He
who loves God with his whole heart and his whole spirit obeys the law,
but with that inventive freedom which marks out what is essential from
what is secondary—a contingent and often groping process. Jesus' consent to the will of the Father is so intimate and so direct that all his
behaviour radiates a personal authority; and for his disciples, impressed by that authority and spiritual freedom, he becomes *the* model.

To return to the human experience of fatherhood: the quasi-legal term 'paternity' seems formal, juridical and repressive, especially in the present cultural climate where man, enclosed in a particularly complex society, cherishes the utopian dream of a spontaneous, primitive and anarchical existence, but on the condition that he does not lose the benefits of society as it is. We should remember, too, that the Church as an institution, in accordance with the model of modern societies, has tended to ordain in a legalistic manner moral, cultic and social behaviour, to the extent even of putting forward the image of a repressive system of laws. These circumstances conceal a fundamental truth: fatherhood is a function of humanization by virtue of the administration of law. It is important to realize the difference between law-making and law-giving. The first suggests the arbitrary nature of the law as imposed by one who wishes his personal authority to prevail, and to do so to the benefit of his power and glory. Under the influence of simplistic notions of human emancipation, it is this interpretation that often attaches to the idea of fatherhood. Psychological research has shown, however, that the absence of a father exercising his fatherhood by law-giving is deeply disturbing to a child. That is obvious. A father who does not put forward rules of life does not really interest a child. He shows that he is indifferent to what will become of the child. Law-giving is part of fatherly love, because it displays wishes about the child's future. If man were only a creature of nature, he would be subject to forms of biological determinism. But to be human, he must become so by forming himself in accordance with goals whose principles are enunciated by the father. The mother also fulfils this function. But it is a function proper to the father in the realm of differentiated relations. Inevitably, for that reason, a child has an ambivalent relation to the father. Human tendencies are chaotic and contradictory. To form himself and to live in the necessary security, a child needs the paternal law. But the law arouses resistance and rebellion. Yet if it, in its own way, acknowledges the father's love as intending for the child's future, rebellion is a 'happy fault'.

This psychological excursus helps us to understand the connexion between Christianity and the moral law as displayed by Jesus when subverting the law through love of the Law. Before all else, the bond of paternity gives the moral law its significance as a bestowal of the Father. That is the meaning of the Father's will, which is at one and the same time an offer of his presence and glory and a condition for enjoying it. Hence the meaning of the law as the Father's will is understandable only inasmuch as man, following Christ, can say to God, in the first person and with all the sincerity of his whole existence: 'Thank you, Father . . .' and 'Your will be done'.

It follows too that Christian ethics, not being subject to the abstract nature of an ideal law, is progressive. The paternal will is a wish and a project for the future of man. In summoning man to the bond of son-hood God invites him to progress and discovery. Too prone to conceive faith as adherence to revealed truths about God, one tends to decide between belief and unbelief. Consequently morality is put forward as a codified set of laws. It would be more in accordance with the essence of practical Christianity to offer models. 'I am the way, the truth and the life' implies that the believer accedes gradually to Life by following the way of Christ as indicated by various evangelical models of life.

A third consequence, bound up with the second, is that creative freedom is the mark of Christian morality. The famous 'love and do what you will' of St Augustine summarizes the nature of that love admirably. He who loves to the extent that he loves does what he wishes inasmuch as he wants to; he desires to love and to accord with the love received.

Empirical research has shown that for many priests faith in God the Father remains a vague general religious idea of providential goodness. It is juxtaposed uneasily with the other idea of God as the judge before whom men have to answer for good and evil. Young men preparing for the priesthood significantly leave out any reference to the paternal function of law-giving. For them God is essentially a religious experi-ence of closeness and trust. In other words, faith is then a process of looking for gratification. That is certainly an essential part of any reli-gion. But if one goes no further than that, there is no access to the intersubjective relation of a love which implies commitment to a form of gradual reciprocity. The difference between faith as 'religious expe-rience' and faith as entry into divine sonhood is analogous to the dis-tance between love as sentiment and commitment in love as an engage-ment for all one's future life. The basis and meaning of Christian morality are not so easily reconciled. The severance between divine fatherhood and, on the other hand, law and judgment, certainly ex-plains the wavering in some sermons between a somewhat pietistic exposition of divine goodness and a far too intrusive form of moralizing.

## Fatherhood and the Future of Mankind

By establishing his Fatherhood, God joins himself to man for all time. The essence of love is a promise of loyalty. Love requires to be loved in that ultimately personal address to the other which is a desire to live by finding the ultimate meaning of life in love. But only He who is the source of life knows how to love with a love which is stronger than death. The fatherhood of God, as it is demonstrated in Christ, implies that which lies beyond death. Moreover it is as the first among brothers, in divine sonhood, that the Father raised up the one whom he had fully endowed with his paternal love. This eschatological project of the Father does not put any new content into ethics. But it does offer a spiritual freedom which is an inspiration and a safeguard for true human morality. And in the cultural history of the West it was in eras when that eschatological faith was alive that Christianity was able to bring about a spiritual revolution in mankind. Just think of the first Christians in the Roman empire, the humanism of the authentic monks, and the achievement of Francis.

All morality is directed to a certain notion of man. It suggests a gradual perfection of man yet contests that affirmation by criticizing what is destructive of the quality of life: passion, spiritual error, the malfunctioning of social and economic bodies. An ethic always stirs men to free themselves from oppressive powers, whether internal or external. It tries to mark out the forces of alienation and also to decide the real freedom which will make man ultimately a self-harmonious and happy being. Whatever it may be, morality is a guide to the perfection of man. Yet that belief in human perfectibility is both a necessary goal to achieve an ever-greater degree of humanity, and an insidious danger. When morality separates from its religious ground and retains the ideal of perfection, that ideal is projected on an historical future defined by reason. If there is nothing beyond human history the ideal of perfectibility has to be sought with the aid of earthly coordinates. Two dangerous procedures are then possible. Because it realizes the actual imperfect state of things, the will to change is grossly dissatisfied. Tradition is criticized and cast aside, and so is any form of authority, for both are seen as responsible for the lack of happiness and harmony. The dream of permanent revolution is kept alive, even though no one knows where to go despite the firm desire first to erase the traditional system in the vague belief that a new mankind will arise from the ashes as if from some aboriginal combustion.

Some even go so far as to justify present immorality by referring their morality to an indefinite future. Some believe that they can mark out the mechanisms and faults which lead to human alienation and offer a rational plan and strategy for freeing man and perfecting him. Technical rationalization is made to serve change and to produce a major effort for the humanization of the individual and society. Hence Marxism as the plan for a perfect humanism has acted as the major reference-system for a number of unbelievers who wished to speed human and social change. The deception and the revulsion they have shown in the face of the actual barbarism of the totalitarian systems is well-known. What is important is to see that the ideology of a perfected mankind, and the belief that one can discern and control the powers of oppression, necessarily changes society into a Gulag.

The temptation to force man to be good is not absent from church history. In our own time it has recurred in a number of sects whose recruitment techniques, wicked psychological manipulations of guilt, oppressive and obfuscating indoctrination, and authoritarian pretensions to prophetic inspiration evidence the apparatus of intellectual and moral compulsion which a religion may be tempted to use when it thinks it has the notion of a complete morality. By identifying itself with the fatherhood from which the law comes, it flouts the essential rules of ethics.

Faith in God the Father has a critical virtue which safeguards morality. The Father is the bestower of the promise and of the law. The meaning of human history lies outside the world. History has a meaning for faith in the Father; but that meaning is withdrawn from man. The word of promise is a break in the human design to settle in theory and in practice the meaning of the human venture. It continues to depend on God's destiny for the world. In faith we know that that destiny will be a glorious transformation which will complete the perfectibility of man. We know too that the historical effort made by mankind is not in vain: faith is a 'power'. But in confirmed ignorance about perfect humanity, and powerless to establish ideal humanity, and trusting in the promise, man relaxes his 'tension', surrenders his exaggerated will to do good, and rejoices at the actual spark of peace, love and well-being that he is able to coax into being. The gospel parables represent a lesson in eschatological hope, and have as their general topic the hidden nature of the Kingdom of God. There is no point in rooting out the tares if we do not at the same time gather the wheat. The everyday world of work, joy and well-being is a sign of the Kingdom, elusive but universally potent and advancing towards the fulness of time. But these everyday things only stand for the Kingdom and the experience of them only supports hope in terms of their present value for men. A world of anguish would no longer be a sign and men would have to humanize it before it becomes one. The symbolic power that hope imparts to the world of men frees it from that destructive violence born of a desire to bring about the heavenly Jerusalem here on earth.

## Love Your Enemies

This is undoubtedly the hardest of all the commandments. It is also the most specifically Christian among them. It introduces conformity to divine Fatherhood into relations with others. It marks out Jesus' disciples from publicans and pagans: 'Do not be like them, for your Father knows what you need before you ask him . . .' (Mt. 6:8). This keynote is recalled in the prayer to the Father that Jesus gave his disciples as a distinctive rule of prayer. It includes only two demands: first the request for bread (which probably has the real meaning of everyday life and a symbolic reference to the morrow of eschatological hope. For Jesus the two are never separate); and the request for fatherly forgiveness which is conditioned by forgiveness of others, one's enemies.

Is this a moral rule? Here again I would say that it is a commandment which goes beyond the strict bounds of morals but which introduces into life an attitude which supports and inspires moral action. True forgiveness is the real essence and means of love. Forgiveness refuses to judge and represents an act of confidence in the secret possibilities of the other's goodness. This specifically evangelical commandment goes beyond the mere quality of goodness. It is the acceptance of God's fatherly attitude to man.

Before all else, forgiveness or love of one's enemies implies a refusal of any intention to identify the other with evil. Forgiveness removes the other's guilt while acknowledging that he is not essentially the source of evil. The petition 'Father, forgive them for they know not what they do' is a translation of the Christian relation to evil. Evil is a great enigma in the world; it is the inconceivable reality, and the totalitarian ideologies or sects that claim to be able to master it tend to play it down. Victory over evil is part neither of theoretical knowledge nor domination of the will, but of hope dependent on faith in God the Father.

True forgiveness is also an act of faith in man's future. It is not possible really to forgive without ceasing to look on oneself as the centre, or without confidence that man, however detestable he may be humanly speaking, is still under the influence of the hidden Kingdom of God.

Something that Freud says in his work on sickness in civilization bears witness that this commandment is not a natural humanist attitude. For Freud it is the unacceptable demand of evangelical morality whose nobility he nevertheless emphasizes along with its ability to attain to a happiness impossible in the merely human order. But Freud also says that too many men are not worthy of one's love. To love them would be to devalue life and to help its degradation. Nevertheless, the ethics of Freudian psychoanalysis shows an exceptional degree of respect for man as the victim of so many unconscious suasions to do evil. But the radical demand for forgiveness goes beyond humanist respect and tolerance. That forgiveness is possible only if man includes in his attitude to his enemies the attitude of the Father who, with infinite discretion, goes out to the prodigal son in order to welcome his return with joy, even if his motivation is merely well-being.

Even if the love of one's enemy, being the practice of faith, is not properly speaking a moral decision, it is very fruitful for moral behaviour. Nothing is so demoralizing as hatred. Evil undergone yet encompassed by true forgiveness reduces and can even destroy one's disposition to moral behaviour. Unjustly treated, with his expectation of respect or love repulsed, and his trust abused, man looks on humanity as soiled and diseased and he loses that faith in mankind which is necessary for moral action.

People sometimes show naive surprise that religion can become a force of terrifying violence and incredible hatred. They are unaware that religion also represents the ultimate terms of reference for judging good and evil, and that it provides its adherents with their conception of man and of the world. The ideal of mankind which evokes one's love and with which one is able to identify also leads one to oppose and to hate those who are different. The much-quoted pride of the pharisees who were against Jesus is a religious product. Religion can be very dangerous. It can increase the force of man's dark powers. For religion to be a source of moral change it has to convert to that patient, discreet and confident love which is the love of God our Father.

In accepting the law as a gift, through the promise which removes perfection beyond human history, and by that love which never judges but forgives and thus preserves faith in man, human morality is able to purify, nourish and creatively renew itself. We are sometimes unhappy that Christian morality has no rules to offer for answering the major questions of social life. But surely it is the responsibility of Christians to discover the best *human* rules for the collective problems of mankind. The Father's will is also that through the given law his sons should reach independence and take on responsibility for their world.

*Translated by V. Green*

Norbert Rigali

# Christ and Morality

THE QUESTION OF CHRIST AND MORALITY IS NOT THE QUESTION
OF THE SPECIFICITY OF CHRISTIAN ETHICS

THE question of whether there is a specifically Christian ethic has
continued to exercise theologians in Europe and America in the wake
of the Second Vatican Council. Although Richard McCormick could
rightly note earlier in the discussion that, according to 'nearly
everyone', 'human morality (natural law) and Christian morality are
materially identical' but formally different,[1] the virtual consensus of the
time was strangely disquieting and failed to lay the question to rest.
The discussion has recently reached the point where a theologian suspects that the recent abundance of literature on the subject is indicative
of theologians' inability to locate adequately the *real* problem.[2]

It is indeed unfortunate that the problem has been formulated for
contemporary theology in the question, Is there a specifically Christian
morality or ethics? The question means, as McCormick's comment
illustrates: Is Christian morality (or ethics) one and the same thing as
human morality (or ethics), or are they two things? The question first
presupposes that 'Christian morality' and 'human morality' are *es-
sences* and then asks whether or to what extent the one essence is
identical with the other. In short, the question itself of whether there is
a specifically Christian ethic is born of a certain metaphysical viewpoint, indeed the static understanding of the classical worldview.

The classical worldview, antedating both the dawn of historical consciousness and the development of philosophical personalism, yielded
its connatural 'faculty psychology', the so-called rational psychology of
the scholastic manuals, and a corresponding essentialistic ethics,
centred on individual acts (exterior actions and interior intentions).

12

*Moralitas essentialis et substantialis* was located in the object or *finis operis* of the individual action, and *moralitas secundaria et accidentalis* was to be found in its circumstances and intention or *finis extrinsecus, finis operantis*.[3]

Generated out of the classical worldview, the question of whether there is a specifically Christian ethic has meant: Does the essence 'Christian morality' contain individual actions and/or intentions that are not included in the essence 'human morality'? Accordingly, Charles Curran expressed his negative answer to the question about a specifically Christian ethic by noting that 'others who have never accepted or even heard of Christ Jesus are able to arrive not only at the same *ethical decisions about particular matters* but are also able to have for all practical purposes the same *general dispositions and attitudes* such as hope, freedom and love for others even to the point of sacrificing self'.[4]

In a later presentation of this thesis, Curran distinguished his own approach to the question from that of some other contemporary theologians. The latter approach uses 'an abstract concept of the metaphysical notion of the human' while his own approach understands the human in 'the actual historical order in which we live', i.e., in the 'historical sense of man existing as created, fallen and redeemed'.[5] Nevertheless, he rightly notes that, inasmuch as both approaches lead to the same conclusion, there are no great 'practical differences' between them.[6] Indeed, it makes little difference which approach is used. Both conceptions of the human being are standard conceptual tools of the classical world-view. Curran's approach is no more within historical consciousness than is the other.

Whereas the classical worldview inclines toward locating morality primarily, if not exclusively, within individual acts, a contemporary worldview sees it as lodged essentially in the totality of the person, i.e., in the unity that is a person's temporal existence. Morality, on this view, is basically in the continuing fundamental option 'between a "yes" and a "no" in which man, as a spirit, unconditionally commits or refuses himself'.[7] Morality is, quintessentially, the person *as person*, i.e., the person in his or her enduring choice 'with respect to the totality of existence, its meaning and its direction'.[8]

At its best, the classical worldview, with its traditional doctrine of the virtues, approximates the contemporary view of morality that locates it primarily in persons and only secondarily in individual acts. Nevertheless, all too frequently the virtues themselves have been understood as only so many different human capacities enabling a person to perform individual acts or to perform them more easily. In any case, introducing a restatement of the traditional doctrine of the virtues into the discussion of whether there is a specifically Christian ethic cannot transform the question itself into being anything other than a question of the classical worldview, which as such can never receive a satisfactory answer today.[9]

It is understandable, then, that the moralist who situates himself or herself within a horizon of historical consciousness responds, when confronted with the question of whether there is a specifically Christian morality, differing from human morality, with a trace of impatience: Of course, there is; in fact, there are many.[10]

The time has come, therefore, for moralists to reject decisively the question focused on specificity, which despite good intentions is at best a form of inverse parochialism. The question for theologians is the wide-open question: What should Christian ethics be today?

Our question here is an aspect of this wide-open question. What can and should Christ mean, if anything, in the moral lives of Christians? This question, of course, can be answered only by answering another, which it presupposes: Who and what is Jesus Christ? From this perspective it is evident that moral theology should be a science that seeks to relate Christology to the moral lives of Christians.[11]

### JESUS IS 'OUR LAW', 'OUR NORM ITSELF'

Jesus as Son of God, as God who is incarnated in him, is the Truth (Jn. 14:6), God's revelation of himself and the divine revelation of the human. Because of his hypostatic union or privileged relation to the Father, because of his being filled with God in a unique way—and not despite this uniqueness—he is God's absolute and definitive revelation of the human. As such, he is the absolute and definitive norm of the *humanum*. He is 'our Law', 'our Norm itself'.[12]

What does it mean that Jesus Christ is our law or norm, the norm of the *humanum*? Two clarifications are needed here: the *humanum* and law or norm.

As traditional theology distinguished between *actus hominis* and *actus humanus,* the *humanum* revealed in Jesus must, of course, be distinguished from a physical or ontic notion of the human being. The revealed *humanum* is *personal* reality.

The *humanum* in this personal or moral sense has always been the object of ethics. However, in the ethics of the classical, prepersonalist worldview there was undeniably a tendency to locate morality primarily in the *actus humanus,* as noted earlier, rather than in the *vita humana.* Accordingly, classical moral theology had no need to distinguish *vita humana* from *vita hominis* in the way in which it distinguished acts and to employ *'vita humana'* as a key concept. The *humanum* revealed in Jesus, nevertheless, must be recognized as the totality that it is, namely, a human life, a personal existence in the world.

It is not enough that the contemporary moralist be explicitly and constantly aware that the *humanum* or *morale* of an act is secondary to and derived from the primary *humanum* or *morale* that is personal existence in the world. Since personal existence is radically and essentially interpersonal and unrestrictedly open in principle to the other, the *humanum,* to be understood and located adequately, must be seen in its ultimate context, the entire human race throughout the past and into the future. In other words, the *humanum* of an act can be seen only in the *humanum* of a life, and the *humanum* of a life exists only in relation to the *humanum* that is the history-in-progress of the human race.

Traditionally in moral theology the term 'law' connotes immediately and directly human acts. In accord with the classical worldview's inclination to see the *humanum* or *morale* primarily in acts is its tendency to understand law as primarily referred to *doing*. Even 'natural law' has frequently seemed to be ultimately no more than a law of doing or not doing when its 'primary precept' was formulated: *bonum est faciendum et prosequendum, et malum vitandum*.[13] On a contemporary view, however, natural law can be clearly seen as referring directly and primarily to human life, personal existence, as the unity and whole that it is rather than to human acts or even the sum-total of human acts. It can be seen as the law of being and becoming; for it is the 'dynamically inviting possibility' confronting human freedom, 'Become what thou art', in which 'man's "self" presents its demands to an "ego" consciously realizing itself'.[14]

That Jesus Christ is the law of morality means that his human life is the standard by which every human life is to be measured. The task of trying to understand Jesus as the norm of the *humanum,* then, is not directly one of collecting his teachings about what people should or should not do—for example, in the Sermon on the Mount. Nor is it directly the effort of trying to discern in Jesus' individual acts and reactions to situations models to be copied or repeated. The task is, rather, that of trying to discern the unity, the unified meaning, of the human life that is Jesus himself. In a word, that Jesus is the norm of the *humanum* means that his meaning, the meaning that he freely gave to his life (or, more precisely, that he freely chose to accept for his life), the meaning that he freely created out of his life—this is the norm of what every *vita humana* should mean.

There is, of course, a great philosophico-theological problem in saying of a particular human life that this is the absolute and definitive norm in history of what every human life should be and mean. Since historicity is of the essence of a human life, to designate a human life as the absolute, definitive norm of the *humanum* in history is to say, paradoxically, that this human life, this historical reality *as such*, transcends all historical reality as its norm or ideal.

We should emphasise the paradox here. It is not paradox but mystery that Christ *as divine* transcends history or that his grace is offered universally to all persons. It is a paradox, however, that Jesus Christ *as human,* as the particular *historical reality* that his human life is, transcends history as its norm. More sharply stated, the paradox is that Jesus Christ *precisely as historical, precisely as humanum,* transcends the *humanum* of history-in-progress; as *humanum,* he is 'the concrete universal'.

A human life can be reasonably believed to transcend history-in-progress as its absolute, definitive norm only if this life is believed to be a revelation of the *humanum* by the absolute God. On the other hand, to believe reasonably (in line with the Catholic tradition that faith is reasonable) that a particular human life is the absolute, definitive norm of the *humanum,* one must be able to perceive in this human life the quality of absoluteness.

### THE ABSOLUTENESS OF JESUS' LIFE IS THE ABSOLUTE NORM OF THE HUMANUM

As Christology in recent years has increasingly emphasized Christology 'from below', some theologians have sought to capture the absoluteness of the humanity of Christ in the phrase, 'the man for others':

> Jesus is 'the man for others', the one in whom Love has completely taken over, the one who is utterly open to, and united with, the Ground of his being. And this 'life for others, through participation in the Being of God', is transcendence . . . Because Christ was utterly and completely 'the man for others', because he *was* love, he was 'one with the Father', because 'God is love'.[15]

In Jesus 'there is nothing of self to be seen, but solely the ultimate, unconditional love of God', which constitutes him absolutely as 'the man for others and the man for God'.[16] Jesus is he who emptied himself in the self-giving love of unconditional commitment to God that grounds his unqualified self-giving love for others (cf. Phil. 2:6–9).

That Jesus is perfectly human means, therefore, that 'his social world is co-extensive with humanity, that he is open to all men and moreover open to all that is in man.'[17] In this sense his life can be seen as 'the coming of a new humanity, a new kind of community amongst men',[18] a humanity that is not restricted by any human particularisms such as race, sex, nation, culture, age, historical period, social conditions or religion (cf. Gal. 3:27–28).

To believe reasonably that Jesus is the absolute norm of the *humanum* is to perceive in his historical existence (as presented in and carried by the tradition of the Christian community) the *humanum* that freely, totally and unconditionally locates itself within and embraces the *humanum* in its ultimate context of the entire human race, history-in-progress.

Since the *humanum* or *morale* is primarily the *vita humana*, not the *actus humanus*, contemporary ethics must understand itself, much more than did traditional moral theology, as a science directly concerned with *vita humana*, which can speak legitimately about the *actus humanus* only in this explict context. The crisis in which moral theology finds itself today should be recognized as nothing less than a crisis of identity. Moral theology can no longer be defined as *'scientia theologica de actibus deliberatis, prout relationem dicunt ad finem ultimum supernaturalem'*[19] or as 'that branch of Theology which states and explains the laws of human conduct in reference to man's supernatural destiny'.[20] Moral theology must redefine itself today as a science of the Christian life and must transform itself into a new kind of science.

A moral theology that is not immediately or directly but only mediately and secondarily about deliberate acts or laws of human conduct must, of course, continue to discuss human acts. It will discover, however, that it has both more and less to say about them than the classical worldview had. More, in the sense that the meaning of an act will have to be seen explicitly in the context of a personal existence located within history. Less, in the sense that, once seen as only a single and limited expression of the *vita humana*, the *actus humanus* frequently requires considerably less attention than moralists are wont to give. The frequently excessive and even obsessive concern with acts of the classical worldview can be seen, for example, in the notion: 'All directly voluntary sexual pleasure is mortally sinful outside of matrimony', 'even if the pleasure be ever so brief and insignificant'.[21] Such a doctrine can be conceived only through a total failure to recognize that *vita humana*, not *actus humanus*, is the primary locus of the *humanum* and, therefore, of morality.

*Vita humana (vita personalis, vita moralis)* is a reality far greater than acts or the sum-total of acts. *Vita humana* is, for example, a vocation, a profession, a marriage, the "causes" to which one commits oneself, the organizations to which one belongs, a 'life-style' and much more. Above all, *vita humana* is a network of personal relationships and a developmental process involving many different stages of personal growth. All this and more is the *vita humana* that must be the focal point of the new moral theology of the future.

To believe that Jesus is the authentic, definitive *humanum* is to accept the difficult truth expressed by his life: 'The man who loves his life loses it, while the man who hates his life in this world preserves it to life eternal' (Jn. 12:25). It is to accept the paradox that self-fulfillment is found in history in the sign of the Cross (cf. Gal. 6:14), that self-fulfillment is the agapeic life that empties itself even unto death on a cross in order to be completely for God and others.

The Cross, however, is not only the primary Christian symbol of life and love. It is also the fundamental Christian symbol of sin—the absurd, the mystery of evil, defying rational explanation. Because the Cross is a symbol of the absurd, human reason alone cannot unambiguously recognize its glory, the fulfillment that it represents (cf. 1 Cor. 1:23). Similarly, because the authentic *humanum* in history is under the sign of the Cross, unaided human reason cannot find its way unequivocally to the knowledge that the norm of the *morale* is a life of self-emptying love for others even unto the Cross. Only by reason of the historical contingency of a sin-filled, absurdity-affected world can love mean the Cross and the Cross mean love.

As a creation of God and ontologically good, the human person is a being capable of self-understanding. To the extent, however, that human nature is wounded by sin, the human person is subject to a sin-generated darkness of intellect—that is not simply a natural absence of perfect knowledge, but a darkness participating in absurdity—which impedes self-understanding and an understanding of the norm of self-fulfillment.

Moreover, that Jesus is the norm of the *humanum* is reasonable belief, not purely rational knowledge. If Jesus is this absolute, definitive norm, he is so only in virtue of God's free choice to reveal himself in the historical reality of Jesus. God's free act of self-communication in history, however, cannot be known through purely philosophical knowledge.

For these reasons, then, it is understandable that philosophical ethics or other traditions have often presented as the norm of the *humanum* something other than the life of self-emptying, unrestricted love for others. It is understandable also that the norm of the *humanum* that emerges from traditional moral theology cannot unequivocally be said to be this agapeic life under the sign of the Cross. Traditional moral theology, created within the classical worldview, constructed its morality basically upon the rational necessities that flowed from its understanding of natural law. Only with the dawn of an historical consciousness replacing the classical worldview can it seem even conceivable that ethics is ultimately based on an *historical* reality, the *humanum* that is Jesus. But can ethics ultimately be based on an historical reality?

As noted above, to believe reasonably that Jesus is the absolute norm of the *humanum* or *morale,* one must perceive the quality of absoluteness in his life. In other words, 'Jesus is recognized as the Christ because he has brought to fulfillment the deepest moral aspirations of mankind'.[22] Of course, interior grace is required for the assent of faith, but this assent is also in virtue of the 'natural law' of the deepest moral aspirations of mankind, enabling one to perceive the absoluteness of Jesus' life.

Does this mean that Jesus, the life of Jesus, is ultimately measured by this 'natural law'? The law of the deepest moral aspirations of humanity is the law of our concrete nature, not *natura pura,* in the order of salvation. It is the law of a nature intrinsically affected and transformed by the supernatural existential. What the natural law would be for a humanity in the state of *natura pura,* we are unable, in the final analysis, to know with precision and certitude; such a natural law is a remainder-concept, a *Restbegriff.* The law of our concrete nature, however, is a law of humanity's supernatural destiny, the destiny that it has through Christ, the Son of God. Our 'natural law', the law of humanity's deepest moral aspirations in history, the law of our concrete, supernaturally affected nature, exists through Christ. He is the measure of our 'natural law' (cf. Col. 1:15–17).

Christian can accept Jesus as the absolute norm of the *humanum* or *morale* in his or her own life only by believing that Jesus is the norm for all, not only Christians. What characterises Christianity with regard to morality is that the *morale* is the *humanum,* precisely this and nothing more. In the order of salvation, the human being, in virtue of his supernaturally affected nature, is the potentiality for personal self-transcendence in the absolute mystery of the personal God through self-emptying, self-giving love for others. The authentic *vita humana,* a possibility for all through the universal offer of divine grace, is the fulfillment of this potentiality. This is what the God who is incarnated in Jesus Christ means for morality.

## Notes

1. Richard A. McCormick, 'Notes on Moral Theology', *Theological Studies* 32 (1971), pp. 74–75.

2. Tadeusz Styczen, "Autonome und christliche Ethik als methodologisches Problem," *Theologie und Glaube* 66 (1976), pp. 211–19.

3. H. Noldin-A. Schmitt, *Summa theologiae moralis,* 27th edit. (Innsbruck, 1940), I:78; B. H. Merkelbach, *Summa theologiae moralis* (Bruges, 1956), I:139–40.

4. Charles E. Curran, "Is There a Distinctively Christian Social Ethic?" in *Metropolis: Christian Presence and Responsibility,* Philip D. Morris, ed. (Notre Dame, 1970), pp. 115–16. Emphasis added.

5. Charles E. Curran, "Is There a Catholic and/or Christian Ethic?" *Proceedings of the Twenty-Ninth Annual Convention: The Catholic Theological Society of America* 29 (1974), pp. 144–45.

6. *Ibid.,* 146.

7. Louis Monden, *Sin, Liberty and Law* (New York, 1965), p. 31 (*Vernieuwd Geweten,* Bruges 1964).

8. *Ibid.*

9. I have in mind here especially James M. Gustafson, *Can Ethics Be Christian?* (Chicago/London, 1975).

10. Cf. Daniel C. Maguire, 'Catholic Ethics with an American Accent', in *America in Theological Perspective,* Thomas M. McFadden, ed. (New York, 1976), pp. 14–15.

11. The index of a traditional moral theology manual, e.g., Noldin-Schmitt, need not list 'Jesus,' 'Christ' or 'Lord.' Bernard Häring's *The Law of Christ* radically transforms the manualist tradition.

12. Bernard Häring, *The Law of Christ* (Westminister, 1961), I:234 (*Das Gesetz Christi,* Freiburg im Br., 1959).

13. Ia IIae, q. 94, a. 2.

14. L. Monden, *op. cit.,* p. 88.

15. John A. T. Robinson, *Honest to God* (Philadelphia, 1963), p. 76. A better expression of the absoluteness of Jesus would be 'the person for others'.

16. *Ibid.,* 74, 77.

17. Herbert McCabe, *What Is Ethics All About?* (Washington/Cleveland, 1969), p. 129.

18. *Ibid.*

19. F. Hurth and P. M. Abellan, *De principiis, de virtutibus et praeceptis* (Rome, 1948), I:7.

20. Henry Davis, *Moral and Pastoral Theology* (New York, 1938), I:1.

21. Heribert Jone, *Moral Theology,* trans. by Urban Adelman (Westminster, 1956), p. 146.

22. John Macquarrie, *Three Issues in Ethics* (New York-Evanston-London, 1970), p. 85.

Pierre-Thomas Camelot

# God, a Spirit Who Makes One Live

## THE SPIRIT IS LIFE

'A LIFE-GIVING Spirit' is the phrase in I Cor. 15:45, where the first Adam, 'a living being', is opposed to the last Adam, 'a life-giving spirit'.[1] In what sense is this 'life-giving Spirit' a specific ground of Christian behaviour?

St Paul's words make us look again at the narrative of man's creation (Gen. 2:7): after having moulded man's body the Creator breathes into him the breath of life, the 'spirit' which makes him a living being. Man is endowed with a living soul by participating in the life of the living God. This is the comment of Irenaeus (*Adv. Haer.* II,54,3) who adds that by communion in the Spirit of the Father, man is no longer *carnal*, but *spiritual* (V, 6,1; 9,2. Cf. I Cor. 2:15; 3:1). Man is only *perfect* when moved by the Spirit of God. Later Gregory of Nyssa would say: 'He who is not moved by the Spirit is not a human being'.[2] God is Spirit, and man's life in all its manifestations, from *psychè* to *pneuma,* is only given him through participation in the Spirit of God, a 'life-giving Spirit'.

The life-giving Spirit is not an anonymous and impersonal force, like the blowing wind (cf. John 3:8). If the personality of the Holy Spirit has only been revealed gradually (cf. Greg. Naz., *Theol. Orations,* V, 6), it had already been suggested by the formulae used by Paul and John (Rom. 8:11; 16:26; John 14:15, 26; 16:15, etc.). Early on Irenaeus, when speaking of the 'two hands of the Father', clearly meant that, like the Son, the Spirit is a living Person (*Adv. Haer.* IV,20,1; V,6,1; 28,4).

But this brings in a theology of the Trinity. If the operations *ad extra* are common to the three Persons, doesn't each of them, each of the 'two hands', have its own function in this unique action, the work of

21

our salvation? The formulae used by St Paul seem to suggest this. Thus Ephesians 2:18 says: to (*pros*) the Father through (*dia*) the Son in (*en*) the Spirit. Or in II Cor. 13:14: the Spirit works this communion of the believers in the love (agapè) of the Father through the grace of the Lord Jesus Christ.

The life of the Father is communicated to a Christian through Christ in the Spirit. Here we must quote St Athanasius where he sums up long pages saturated with Scripture: 'As the Father is the source, and the Son is called the river, we are said to drink the Spirit' (*Ad Serapion*, I:19). Gregory of Nyssa puts it in more technical terms: 'Any action coming from God and ending up in the creature . . . starts from (*ek*) the Father, proceeds through (*dia*) the Son and is completed in (*en*) the Spirit' (*Ad Ablabium*, P.G. 45, col. 125). This 'life of the Spirit' (or in the Spirit) which bears the fruit of sanctity is imparted in baptism.[3] The life-giving Spirit is the Spirit received in baptism, whose anointment penetrates the spirit of the new convert as He poured his anointment over Jesus at his baptism in the Jordan.[4]

Thus baptism 'in the name of the Lord Jesus' is also a baptism in the Spirit; in the same way the Holy Spirit, Spirit of God, is also the Spirit of Christ. It would be easy to gather texts of St Paul where these words occur.[5] Raised from the dead through the power of the Spirit (Rom. 1:4; cf. 8:11), Jesus in his turn sends the Spirit. This is because the Spirit 'proceeds' from the Father *and* the Son (or from the Father *through* the Son), and the 'mission' derives from this 'procession': thus Jesus promises the Spirit, he sends the Spirit (John 14:26; 15:26; 16:7, etc.), and gives the Spirit when he has been glorified through his death and resurrection (John 7:39; 19:30, 34; 20:22). In return this gift of the Spirit radiates the glory of him who is risen; he is 'the presence in us of the glory of the Lord who transforms us into his likeness'.[6]

'Transformed into his likeness'; thus one can say that the Spirit moulds us into the likeness of Christ. This likeness is not simply an imitation of a model external to us, and it is therefore better to say that the Spirit who acts from within, *forms Christ in us*. Paul said it twice over: we have received the Spirit who makes adoptive sons of us (Rom. 8:15; Gal. 4:6. See also, e.g., Basil, *De Spiritu Sancto* 15, 36). It is a profound transformation, at the core of our being, making us 'a new creation' in the Spirit (cf. II Cor. 5:17; Gal. 6:15). And again: '. . . we are being changed into his likeness . . . through the Lord who is Spirit' (II Cor. 3:18).

Thus Paul can say: 'For me to live is Christ' (Phil. 1:21); 'It is no longer I who live, but Christ who lives in me' (Gal. 2:20). But also: 'The law of the Spirit who gives life . . . in Jesus Christ' (Rom. 8:2); 'But if Christ is in you, . . . the Spirit is your life' (Rom. 8:10–11). 'To be in

Jesus Christ' (Rom. 8:1) and 'to live by the Spirit' (Gal. 3:25) is one and the same reality. 'He who is united to Christ is one spirit with him' (I Cor. 6:17). One is tempted to use a capital letter here: 'one Spirit'!

One might also say without forcing the parallel that the Spirit who forms Christ in the Christian is the same Spirit who wrought the incarnation of the Son of God (cf. Luke 1:35). Did not a true Christian mystic ask that the Spirit should 'come upon her' (the words used by Luke) in order that 'as it were an incarnation of the Word' would take place in her soul?[7] Through the Spirit Christ lives in her and 'makes her soul identify with all the movements of his (Christ's) soul'.[8] In particular, the Spirit fashions Christ's own prayer in the Christian; or better, he himself 'cries' that prayer within the soul (Rom. 8:4; Gal. 4:7); it is the first law of Christian prayer: with Christ, in the Spirit, to the Father (cf. Ignatius of Antioch, *Rom.* 7,2; see also Paul, Eph. 2:18). But here we reach the basic law of Christian conduct and the real subject of this article. Some aspects of it have to be explained.

### THE SPIRIT SETS MAN FREE AND MAKES HIM NEW

The Spirit who moulds Christ in the Christian and makes him act as a son of God (cf. Rom. 8:14) is a *Spirit of newness*. The prophets had already announced the messianic era as marked by the effusion of pure water (the Spirit) and the gift of a new heart and a new spirit. The new covenant is a covenant in the Spirit (Ez. 11:19–20; 36:25–7). Through the Spirit sent by him who is risen, poured out at the Pentecostal event, and conveyed through the washing of regeneration (Titus 3:5), the Christian is a new creation (II Cor. 5:17; Gal. 6:13), a new man (Ephes. 2:15; 4:24), who lives and acts ('walks') in a renewed life (Rom. 6:24), which is a renewal of the spirit (Rom. 7:6).

'I make all things new' (Rev. 21:5). But new with regard to what? What kind of a past? Here one can only refer again to the Epistle to the Romans (8:1 and 16) which says everything that is essential. Whether one looks at Christian behaviour from the point of view of its inner principle or from that of the law imposed from outside, everything is new here. The new man no longer 'walks *according to the flesh*'. By 'flesh' we should here understand the meaning given to it by St Paul: man wounded by sin in all his vitality. But the Spirit who gives life in Jesus Christ has freed man from the law of sin and death (8:2). Released from the hold the flesh has over him, the Spirit of God—the Spirit of Christ—urges him on towards life and peace (8:6, 14). In so far as what interests us here more immediately is concerned, one realizes that the Spirit 'dwells in' the Christian (8:9, 11) and animates him from within. Here full value is given to the biblical images of the life-giving *breath,* or the *heart,* as well as of the living water which springs up and murmurs within. The inner law (see below), the law of Christian conduct is demanding and requires that one is open to and ready to comply with the Spirit, silence and purity of heart, all of which means that one lets 'the works of the flesh die' (8:13; cf. Rom. 6:6: 'the old man has been crucified so that the sinful body might be destroyed'). No doubt, the Spirit who makes us live a new life is the Spirit of the risen Jesus Christ, but he was first crucified (cf. Gal. 5:24, and again, see below).

There is also newness with regard to the *letter* and the *law.* Moses' law, written 'on tables of stone' (cf. II Cor. 3:3), and holding man captive under the yoke of observances, unable to justify him (cf. Rom. 3:20), is replaced by the law of the Spirit, 'written on tables of flesh', in the *heart* (cf. again II Cor., *ibid.*). These images express in their turn the internal nature of the law of the Spirit, of life according to the Spirit (cf. Jer. 31:33; Ez. 35:25–27). Moreover—and this must be stressed here—the new life in the Spirit is a law of *freedom* (cf. James 1:25; 2:12). For, animated by the Spirit from within, the Christian does not act under the constraint of a law which remains external to him but in the spontaneity of love. The law by which a Christian acts is far from being a morality of slavery and fear (cf. Rom. 8:15; Gal. 4:7) or a 'closed' morality; it cannot confine itself to the limits of what is allowed and what is forbidden. The new law in the Spirit is a law of dynamism and progress. Since it is the Spirit who 'drives' the son of God (cf. Rom. 8:14), he must always press on (cf. Phil. 3:13). One can consider a legal observance as over and done with but one has never done with the urge of the Spirit who beckons us to go beyond ourselves, 'to cross to the other shore' (cf. Mk. 4:35). When all the commandments have been observed there is still always something lacking (cf. Mk. 10:21).

The son of God is therefore led by the Spirit who dwells in him (Rom. 8:9). He acts on his own, freely, moved by the law of the Spirit of life, a law which is within him. Here one should recall Thomas Aquinas who, prompted by St Paul and St Augustine (*De Sp. et Litt.,* 17, 29, above all 21, 36; P.L. 44, 218 ff., and 222), wrote this astonishing passage with his usual simplicity. In it he compared the old Law with the new Law of the Gospel: 'What is most important in the law of the New Testament and gives it all its force is the very grace of the Holy Spirit which is given through belief in Christ. Therefore the New Law is *principaliter* the very grace of the Holy Spirit, which is given to those who believe in Christ' (Ia IIae, 106,1). 'Principally' must not be understood as referring to something else that would be secondary, but as *in principle.* The principle by which a Christian acts is the grace of the Spirit, 'a life-giving God'. Enlivened from within by the Spirit, the Christian does not act under the constraint of the law but with the freedom of a son, the freedom of love. The law by which a Christian acts is therefore a law that springs from within, and man's whole effort must be to strive at making the law *more internal* under the impulse of the Spirit.

And so, if the Spirit himself joins our spirit in bearing witness that we are sons of God, and if he himself prompts our prayer (cf. Rom. 8:16, 26), it is he also who unites himself to us in order to make us act, no longer simply in some human way at the cost of much labour and however imperfectly, but with the spontaneity and one might say the suppleness of an 'instinct'. To use an image familiar to those who are spiritually inclined, it is a matter of replacing laborious rowing by spreading one's sail to the breath of the Spirit. Here one meets the classical teaching about the 'gifts', so soundly worked out by St Thomas and his commentators (John of St Thomas), where theological thought gives a marvellous explanation of the experience of those who are moved by the Spirit.[9] These 'spiritual' men and women are not primarily those endowed with exceptional 'charisma' but rather those whose internal life has been enlivened and transformed by the Spirit and his gifts. It seems to me that this theology could throw a great deal of light on the experience of the Spirit which today's 'charismatic' renewal is acquainted with.

## SURRENDER TO THE SPIRIT, LAXISM, PASSIVITY AND THE DISCERNMENT OF SPIRITS

The new Law therefore is an internal law—the Holy Spirit himself, who dwells in the believer—a law of freedom. But both Paul and Peter already warn us not to let the 'flesh' get a hold under the pretext of freedom, and not to turn this freedom into a screen behind which we can hide our evil (Gal. 5:2; I Peter 2:16). Here there is a long history of 'spiritual' movements which, from the beginning (Nicolaitians, certain gnostics, Montanists, and so on), ended up with some strange perversions. Why should this have happened? One could no doubt see in this the result of a dualistic anthropology where the 'flesh' (understood in its most carnal sense), rejected, even cursed, takes revenge: if the flesh is of no importance whatever it can be allowed anything. And one thinks of the Paulicians, the Cathari, the Brethren of the Free Spirit or Molinos. And so the external law keeps its value and remains necessary: it is a discipline (cf. Gal. 3:24) which trains the Christian for this life in the freedom of the Spirit. This 'written' law disposes Christian to receive the grace of the Spirit and teaches him to live under his influence. As long as the Christian is not wholly freed from the 'flesh' in order to give himself totally to the Spirit, the law itself, under the aspect of the 'letter' of the law, remains necessary to remind him of the demands of the law of the Spirit and to make it possible for him to live in true freedom. Recent ecclesiastical texts which, without in any way separating them, distinguish between 'obligation' and 'vital necessity',[10] clearly show what we say here, following St Thomas (*ibid.*): He who is perfect obeys with complete spontaneity, without the need for a law which tells him what he has to do (cf. IIa IIae, 186,5,2m). But is one ever perfect? When has one ever achieved total spiritual freedom (cf. Gal. 5:16–8) under the influence of the Spirit? The humble practice of the virtues is the best way of preparing oneself for the reception of the Spirit (cf. Ia IIae, 68,8,2m).

These thoughts may produce the elements for an answer to a question which historians or theologians cannot fail to ask themselves. 'God, a Spirit who makes us live' and act? A Christian must therefore listen to the Spirit in an attitude of openness and readiness. But must this go so far as passiveness? Here one catches sight of 'the ever latent and dangerous mirage' of 'quietist inaction'[11] and the disturbing figures of Mme Guyon or even Molinos. But the ambiguity of the vocabulary ('indifference', passiveness . . .) should not mislead us, no more than the frequently used image of an 'instrument struck by the Spirit' (cf. Gregory of Nazianzus, *Or.* 43,67; 12,1; *P.G.* 36,585; 35,384). In fact, moved by the Spirit who "helps us in our weakness" (Rom. 8:26), this instrument is far from being merely passive. Without relating the activity displayed by those who are described as 'spiritual'—to mention only two names, a Catherine of Sienna or a Theresa of Avila who, however much given up to the influence of the Spirit who increased their potential for action, retained full clarity of mind and self-control—the history and experience of the saints patently show that this 'passiveness' is terribly demanding. The illusion and the error would lie in letting oneself go down, under the pretext of remaining passive under the impulse of the Spirit, to a veritable 'destruction of psychic life' and to a moral laxism which would justify every kind of laziness and fantasy, even to the point of the worst aberrations.

When St. Paul writes that 'it is God . . . who puts both the will and the action into us' (Phil. 2:13), he does not mean by this that we only have 'to let things happen to us' in complete passivity; in the previous sentence he had already said: 'Work for your salvation in fear and trembling'. And when, after describing the 'fruit of the Spirit' in detail, he says that for those, led by the Spirit, there is no law, he immediately adds: 'Those who belong to Christ Jesus have crucified the flesh with its passions and desires' (Gal. 5:22–23). When one wants 'to live by the Spirit' and 'to walk guided by the impulse of the Spirit', one has to accept the need for what one can only call *asceticism*. The cross dominates the horizon of all Christian life and above all the life according to the Spirit. It was on the cross that the dying Christ 'gave up the Spirit'

(John 19:30). This does not mean a morbid seeking out of suffering nor contempt of the 'flesh', but quite simply the Christian experience: the 'passions' and the desires of the 'flesh' hamper the freedom of the Spirit. Paul treats his body harshly and subdues it, lest he should himself be disqualified in the struggle of the Spirit (cf. I Cor. 9:27). Anyway, one admits freely that a certain kind of Christian speech which expresses a tradition which, too, has its nobility, betrays here a mentality which is unconsciously impregnated with Platonism or Manicheism, and alien to the gospel. 'It kills me, I kill it', said a desert monk when speaking about his body (Dositheus, in *Hist. Laus.*, II,2).

Thus *discretion*, 'the mother of virtues' (St Benedict, *Reg. mon.*, 64; cf. Cassian, *Conf.* II,2 who simply transmits the experience of the 'old men' of the desert), not only makes one check the excesses of an intemperate asceticism but also helps to 'discern' in the various trends of a spiritual movement what comes from the Spirit, what from the 'flesh' and what from the Evil One. The charism of the discernment of the spirits (cf. I Cor. 12:10) is the charism of the masters of the spiritual life, and, in fact, of any Christian who should not 'believe every spirit' (I John 4:1). Living according to the Spirit demands a long and patient training process.

So discretion will gauge what is authentic in the experience to which the spiritual-minded of all ages have borne witness as well as the experience of those who today are involved in the 'charismatic renewal'.[13] Without mentioning more or less extraordinary facts, e.g., the luminous phenomena which one observes among the monks of the desert or St Seraphim of Sarov, or the 'speaking in tongues', what is usually called an 'outpouring of the Spirit' most often makes those who participate not feel anything out of the ordinary but simply the fruits of the Spirit, mentioned by St Paul: love, joy, peace, patience, kindness, gentleness . . . (Gal. 5:22–3), above all peace and joy (cf. Rom. 14:17), frequently accompanied by tears, which, according to those who have experienced it, are also signs of the Spirit. Perhaps our own age has overlooked this too much? The old missals had a special mass *pro petitione lacrymarum*! This peace and joy spring from the only source of that mysterious spiritual unity between the Spirit and our spirit as one experiences it at such a moment.

No doubt, the theologian, like the psychologist or even the sociologist will begin to wonder about this experience which seems to them to be full of ambiguities. Psychological and, indeed, psychosomatic factors may come into it. But why deny that grace can make use of nature, even wounded nature, or that the Spirit can work through human weakness, healing, purifying and transfiguring it? Anyway, a tree is judged by its fruits, and in an experience which, although widespread, is still recent, a witness who, while very sympathetic, means to maintain a critical attitude is free to become aware of genuine fruits of the Spirit.

Finally, a last word which should be developed if one wanted to deal with this topic in full,—and it again contains an element of judgment on the Renewal: 'God, a life-giving Spirit'. It is through the Church and in the Church of Jesus Christ that the Spirit of Christ acts. It is in the communion of the whole Church that a spiritual movement must live and develop. It is in faithfulness to this communion that one can judge its authenticity. The Church is the *locus* of the Spirit: 'Where the Church is, there is the Spirit of God; and where the Spirit of God is there is the Church and all grace, and the Spirit is Truth' (Irenaeus, *Adv. Haer.* III,24,1). 'One has the Holy Spirit according to the degree in which one loves the Church' (Augustine, *In Joann. Tract.*, 22,8).

*Notes*

1. 'The first Adam was an animal being endowed with life, the last Adam was a spiritual being bestowing life.' This T.O.B. translation slightly glosses the text but is accurate.
2. This 'bold formula' is quoted by P. Eudokimov in *Les âges de la vie spirituelle* (1964), p. 83, without reference. I have been unable to trace it.
3. Cf., e.g., Basil of Caesarea, *De Spir. S.*, 35, *P.G.* 32, 129c–132a.
4. Cf., e.g., Cyril (or John) of Jerusalem, *Catech. Myst.*, 3, 1–2 V; for other patristic texts, see my essay 'Spiritualité du baptême' in *Le Baptême du Christ et le baptême du chrétien* (1960), pp. 265–80.
5. Rom. 8:9,11; II Cor. 3:17; Gal. 4:6; Phil. 1:19.
6. J. G. (Guillet) in *Vocabulaire de Théologie Biblique* (2nd ed. 1970), col. 399.
7. *Ecrits spirituels d'Elisabeth de la Trinité* (Coll. La Vigne du Carmel, 1949), p. 81.
8. *Ibid.*, p. 80.
9. See, e.g., P. R. Régamey's synthesis, *Portrait spirituel du chrétien*, 1963.
10. *Pastoral Letter of the bishops to the Catholics of France* (Lourdes, 1976). *Déclaration des évêques de la Région Apostolique de l'Est*, 15 Jan. 1977, in *Doc. Cath.* 6 March 1977, p. 240.
11. J. L. Goré, 'Les grands thèmes de l'Explication des Maximes des Saints: pur amour et état passif', in *Rev. des Sc. Phil. et Théol.*, 1977, p. 21.
12. There is already a vast literature on this subject. I mention here: P. Schoonenberg, 'Le baptême d'Esprit Saint', in *L'Expérience de l'Esprit. Mélanges Schillebeeckx* (1976), pp. 71–96.
13. Cf. A. Vergote, 'L'Esprit, puissance de salut et de santé spirituelle', *ibid.*, pp. 209–23.

Roland Murphy

# Moral Formation

THE OLD Testament, among other things, is literature. Several of its books have become classics or influenced other literary masterpieces. The text of the Hebrew Bible inspires our worship, and authenticates our self-understanding. Significantly, within this literature is enshrined the moral imperatives of our Judaeo-Christian heritage. When one surveys the Law, prophets, liturgy, and wisdom literature, one finds certain ultimates, a life-style which is binding upon those who recognize the Bible as their authority for life.

Perhaps of greater importance is the *experience* of Israel with God, from which the Bible issues. Indeed, the true status of the Bible in our culture is hindered by our inability to imagine a time when it did not exist. Few realize that the Bible was never a household item in any culture until well after the invention of printing. Even among the people of the Bible oral communication was more important than writing. Israel itself had no Bible until the gradual canonization of the Torah, the prophets (earlier and later) and the other writings during the long post-exilic period. It was during this formative period that our models of moral formation were formulated that were later incorporated into the Bible.

While Israel is personified at many points in this essay, it should be understood that the Lord stands behind, and walks with, his people on this long road of moral formation. What is said about Israel is being said about the Lord with whom she covenanted to be a holy people—a people set apart (Ex. 19:6). As his name Yahweh suggests, he will be there, for his people (Ex. 3:12–15).

## THE COVENANT

Surely the covenant relationship between the Lord and his people lies at the heart of Israel's moral formation. Modern research has shown that international suzerainty treaties (between suzerain and vassal) are the analogy by which Israel described her own covenant relationship. The message and even the shape of the book of Deuteronomy follows the form of these treaties; the exhortations, the 'book of the law' (enshrined in chs. 12–26), the blessings and curses.

The stipulations which formed part of the treaties find their counterpart in the law. When Israel rehearsed the covenantal obligations, especially during the feast of the covenant renewal, she was roused to the expression of loyalty which the covenant proclaimed. It is in the liturgy that the Decalogue finds, not its origin, but its proper setting. Both Psalms 15 and 24 reflect this understanding. They are 'entry-liturgies,' that is, a ceremony performed as worshippers presented themselves at the gate of the temple:

> O Lord, who shall sojourn in your tent?
> Who shall dwell on your holy mountain?

The answer to the questions follow:

> He who walks blamelessly and does justice;
> who thinks the truth in his heart
> and slanders not with his tongue;
> who harms not his fellow man,
> nor takes up a reproach against his neighbour . . .
> He who does these things
> shall never be disturbed. (Ps. 15)

Other liturgical celebrations illustrate this kind of emphasis on moral teaching (Psalms 50 and 81):
To the wicked man God says:

> 'Why do you recite my statutes,
> and profess my covenant with your mouth,
> Though you hate discipline
> and cast my words behind you?
> When you see a thief, you keep pace with him,
> and with adulterers you throw in your lot'. (Ps. 50:15–18).

It is in such a covenantal context that the soul of Israel was formed according to the will of her God. One lived in the pressure of this liturgical integrity, of this patient insistence upon the quality of life demanded of those who would worship the Lord.

Another example of the impact of a covenantal relationship can be gathered from a book that is too easily dismissed as merely a collection of ritual laws, namely, Leviticus. There we read the awesome words: 'I, the Lord, am your God,' and 'I am the Lord'. More than a dozen times these weighty words echo throughout the list of moral commands and prohibitions in Lev. 19:

> Speak to the whole Israelite community and tell them:
> 'Be holy, for I, the Lord your God, am holy. Revere your mother and father, and keep my sabbaths. I, the Lord, am your God'.
> (Lev. 10:3–4)

The holiness and otherness of the Lord is recognized in this motivation which undergirds the individual stipulations of the Law.

There is a tendency to decry the emphasis on the Law, which became so characteristic of Judaism in the postexilic period. However, this love for the Law was not legalistic. Any understanding of law can deteriorate into legalism; but respect for the law, a vision of what it expresses, is not legalism. The understanding of the Law as a revelation of the will of God is an admirable and desirable aspect of the Judaeo-Christian heritage. It is significant that the Psalm chosen to introduce the psalter itself speaks of the ideal just person, who 'delights in the law of the Lord, and meditates on his law day and night' (Ps. 1:2). The psalmists put law in its proper context: 'the precepts of the Lord are right, rejoicing the heart' (Ps. 19:9; cf. Ps. 119:16,77).

## THE PROPHETS

At one time it was fashionable to view the prophets as the creators and proponents of ethical monotheism. The uniqueness of the covenant God, with the consequent obligation of fidelity, is not an inaccurate summary of their message. But the implication was that the prophets proposed these ethical ideals for the first time in the context of Yahwism; they were the teachers, not the taught. Today we understand how deeply rooted they were in the traditions of the past. It was the old covenant traditions from which they drew in order to encourage and also to condemn. They were not merely ethically more sensitive than others; all Israel knew the consequences of standing in a covenant relationship. The function of the prophet was to correct and condemn, to call Israel back to covenant fidelity. To this end they cajoled, threatened, and promised, as they stood up against king, priest and (false) prophet.

It was characteristic of them that they would not tolerate a divorce between liturgy and morality, between sacrifice and obedience. They had harsh words for sacrifices, and even for the ark (Jer. 3:16) and the Temple itself (Jer. 7:4), when these were mistakenly interpreted as divine guarantees of national well-being. The honesty and integrity of worship dominates the prophetic approach. There can be no possibility of trading in divine favour; worship must be ethically responsible:

> Trample my courts no more!
>   Bring no more worthless offerings;
>   your incense is loathsome to me . . .
> When you spread out your hands,
>   I close my eyes to you . . .
> Put away your misdeeds from before my eyes;
>   cease doing evil; learn to do good.
> Make justice your aim; redress the wronged,
>   hear the orphan's plea, defend the widow. (Is. 1:13–17)

It was the prophets, in particular, who proclaimed a message of penitence and conversion, a turning back to the Lord. For all the emphasis that is given to sin and doom, the possibility of return was also held out. 'If that nation which I have threatened turns from its evil, I also repent of the evil I threatened to do' (Jer. 18:8; cf. Jon. 3:9–10). Hence Jeremiah was ordered to proclaim to the people of the old Northern Kingdom (destroyed in 721):

> Return, rebel Israel, says the Lord,
>   I will not remain angry with you.
> For I am merciful, says the Lord,
>   I will not continue my wrath forever. (Jer. 3:12)

Amos announced a divine strategy at work for the return of a wayward Israel. This is to say, the adversities suffered by the people were to be seen as trials through which they should learn to repent and return (Am. 4:6; cf. the refrain in 4:8, 10, 11):

> Though I have made your teeth
>   clean of food in all your cities,
>   and have made bread scarce in all your dwellings,
> Yet you returned not to me,
>   says the Lord.

When one surveys the prophetic writings, it is clear that the changing historical circumstances give rise to different emphases. But through it all, there is ongoing formation in moral conduct. Elijah condemns Ahab when Naboth's vineyard is appropriated and Naboth himself is slain (1 Kgs. 21). Amos preaches at the royal sanctuary in Bethel that 'Jeroboam shall die by the sword' (Am. 7:11). Hosea complains that 'there is no fidelity, no mercy, no knowledge of God in the land,' and the threat of the Lord is pronounced: 'The priests shall fare no better than the people; I will punish them for their ways' (Hos. 4:1, 9). To the exiled in Tel-abib, who would complain that they were being punished for the wrongs of others, Ezekiel announces: 'All lives are mine; the life of the father is like the life of the son, both are mine; only the one who sins shall die . . . If he lives by my statutes and is careful to observe my ordinances, that man is virtuous—he shall surely live, says the Lord God' (Ezek. 18:4, 9).

### THE SAGES

A very important source of the moral formation of Israel is the teaching that has been preserved in the wisdom literature: Proverbs, Job, Ecclesiastes, Ecclesiasticus (Sirach), and the Wisdom of Solomon. The sages of Israel were men like Ben Sira and Qohelet, who had followers in a 'school' of some sort (Eccles. 12:9; Sir. 51:23). They articulated a code of conduct that did not always impinge on the ethical. More often than not they were concerned with the 'grey' area: inculcating a sense of responsibility (Prov. 10:26; 27:23–27), warning against laziness (Prov. 10:4; 26:14), urging self-control (Prov. 14:17; 15:1). Sometimes they simply informed their students about 'the way things are': 'All the ways of a man may be right in his own eyes, but it is the Lord who proves hearts' (Prov. 21:2). They taught by means of aphorism and story, but also by admonitions which are as intense as the preaching in Deuteronomy (Prov. 3:1–18). They studiously avoid reference to the central Israelite concepts of covenant, Exodus, Sinai—those distinguishing marks of Israelite salvation history. Nevertheless, matters of the Law often surface in the teaching of the sages (e.g., cp. Prov. 24:23 with Deut. 19:14 and Hos. 5:10). The moral content derives from a wider context than sacral law or covenant stipulation; it comes from the ethos of the people. This is characteristic of the wisdom tradition, which is spectacularly silent about Law and liturgy. It has its foundation in Israel's understanding of nature, of the work of creation. Here she formed the lessons that nature and human experience can offer to human beings. This view of reality is reflected in the separate, discrete, sayings found in Prov. 10–31, as well as in the wisdom poems of Prov. 1–9.

How and when did this literature begin? At one time it was simply accepted that the older wisdom (Prov. 10 ff.) was the achievement of the educated scribes of the court school in Jerusalem. This was suggested by the existence of some 'king' sayings (not very many; cf. Prov. 16:10–15; 25:2–7), and by the remarkable similarity between the sayings and those of the Egyptian 'teachings' (*Sebayit*), which were associated with Egyptian royalty and courtiers. But it stands to reason that Israel did not suddenly acquire wisdom with Solomon and the ensuing cultural ties with Egypt. Rather, we have to look into the traditions handed down within the clan, within the family. It was the tribal elders, the parents, who would have passed on the 'wisdom' which they expected to inform the conduct of their peers and their children. A vivid picture of family wisdom at work is presented in Tob. 4:3–21, in which Tobit, in view of his approaching death, gives a series of admonitions and sayings to young Tobias.

Especially in the area of wisdom there appears the problem of divine retribution. The mystery of the divine conduct was accepted in all levels of Israelite thought, but the issue of divine justice pressed the conclusion that the Lord would reward the good and punish the evil. This thought is central to Deuteronomy as much as to Proverbs. The sages were convinced of the opposition between wisdom and folly, justice and wickedness, and they looked for a corresponding result: adversity and death for the foolish, as opposed to prosperity and life for the wise. But they were also aware of the ambiguities of life, that 'there is no wisdom, no understanding, no counsel, against the Lord' (Prov. 21:30). Hence there is the paradoxical statement of Prov. 3:11–12:

> The discipline of the Lord, my son, disdain not,
>   spurn not his reproof,
> For whom the Lord loves he reproves,
>   and he chastises the son he favours.

Not everyone, however, could live with this paradox. The friends of Job become the spokesmen of the dominant theology that 'defended' the justice of God, but at the expense of his freedom. If Job was suffering, his own wrong-doing had to be the cause. If only Job would turn to God in repentance, he would be healed—Eliphaz offers this dubious consolation to the suffering Job (Job 5). Ecclesiastes admitted that he simply could not make sense out of what God is doing: 'I recognized that man is unable to find out all God's work that is done under the sun, even though neither by day nor by night do his eyes find rest in sleep. However much man toils in searching, he does not find it out; and even if the wise man says that he knows, he is unable to find it out' (Eccl. 8:17)

Seen in the light of these developments, the famous chapter 53 of Isaiah is all the more remarkable. Here is a real breakthrough in the Israelite view of suffering. It is not necessarily tied to wrongdoing. The reader feels the excitement and awe registered in 53:4 ff:

Yet it was our infirmities that he bore,
   our sufferings that he endured,
While we thought of him as stricken,
   as one smitten by God and afflicted.
But he was pierced for our offenses,
   crushed for our sins . . .
The Lord laid upon him
   the guilt of us all.

The suffering of the Servant in Isaiah 53 is seen to be innocent but redemptive of others, healing. This does not 'explain' suffering; it remains a mystery. But one becomes actively engaged in this mystery of suffering as a mystery of life.

This summary of the factors bearing on the moral formation of Israel necessarily leaves many questions unanswered. One of these, which perhaps may have already occurred to the reader, is this: Why did not Israel, as a beneficiary of divine revelation, propose a moral code clearly superior in every respect? Such a question can, of course, be directed to Christianity itself. This question also presumes that moral formation of human beings is simply a matter of edict, of command and prohibition. But here the Bible presents a striking picture of divine condescendence, of divine patience.

Indeed, few demands are edicted which stand out of tune with moral tone of the ancient Near East. There is an implicit acceptance, and therefore adoption, of much of the morality of Israel's neighbors. The relationship between Israelite and Egyptian–Mesopotamian wisdom sayings is one evidence of this. One cannot deny that in Israel there were certain striking absolutes: Yahweh was not imaged or merely worshipped with other gods; he was a jealous god, and hence the official condemnation of sacred prostitution and fertility rites. But the fact remains: there is a remarkable divine tolerance of questionable human behaviour. Perhaps another way of putting this is to say that there was always a cultural conditioning to the moral formation of Israel. The commandments themselves were time-conditioned, and they were continually reinterpreted throughout Israel's history. All this suggests that in the plan of the divine pedagogy the changes in these several areas were to be left to the historical development of an appropriate moral sense.

We have tried to show that behind the literature of the Old Testament lies a process which includes: the liturgy of the covenant renewal, the reprimand of the prophet, and the persuasive insight of the sage which rested on the accumulated wisdom of the community. Together these were aimed at making Israel a suitable partner in the covenant relationship with God. The question remains, is this pertinent to the life of the Church? The symbolism of the breaking of the bread, the words of Jesus, the wisdom of the Epistle of St James, the catechesis of the *Didachē* are all examples of how the moral formation of the Christian people has continued in the tradition of Israel. But have we taken them seriously?

Perhaps we need to reflect again on moral formation in our own day. In recent times some religious educators have questioned the value of 'lessons' imparted through instruction in the context of formal schooling. Instead, they have advocated a return to catechesis of intentional socialization. That is to say: catechesis as a pastoral activity which, while concerned with moral formation, focuses attention on the many formal and informal influences and environments that persons experience within their families and the Church.

If the Bible has any bearing on moral formation, it suggests a total educative process (catechesis), wherein the world view and values of the faith community are transmitted within the family as in the style of the wisdom literature, and sustained by participation in the liturgy of the community, and challenged by the prophetic leadership within which the family and community stand. If Christianity does not take seriously this biblical lesson, it will lose an important insight into the nature of moral formation. Of course, it may be objected that the history of Israel's moral formation is filled with failure, scrupulously recorded in the pages of the Bible. But does not the triumph of the moral formation of the People of God lie precisely in such honesty and clarity?

# PART II

*Does the Specific Nature of the Christian God Have Unique Consequences for Any Form of Moral Training?*

Helmut Juros

# Formation of Conscience and Ethics: Some Methodological Observations

THE central question of the Christian attitude to the formation of conscience is generally more concerned with the motivations of the subject than with any objective reason for moral behaviour. However the empirico-psychological question as to what in fact motivates the Christian's moral action is not such a crucial factor in the Christian approach to the formation of conscience as the specifically ethical question as to what constitutes a moral action. One is thus faced with the genuinely ethical question: what are the objective factors underlying moral behaviour apart from and beyond the subjective motivation of the individual concerned which must influence his conscience, causing him to act in a moral way? Ethics seems to provide various different answers to this fundamental question.

Which ethical approach, theological and philosophical aspects apart, yields the correct answer? In the first place, it must be 'ethical' in the methodological sense, able to grasp the objective merit as well as the obligation arising from it. Only a methodologically-based concept of ethics can reveal the divine concept on which it is based, and thus also the way in which the Christian God constitutes a specific purpose for action on which the Christian formation of conscience may be based. God can only be truly comprehended as the motive for moral action if the underlying reason is easily grasped. Without this, the morally obligating code of behaviour would be incomprehensible. Hence the position of God, in effect the whole question of theology, introduces a further methodological problem into any ethical discussion of the Christian formation of conscience. This article will attempt to examine these methodological problems and perhaps bring us closer to a clarification.

The problem of the formation of conscience was not invented by Christian theologians. It is not a specifically Christian issue; nor was it invented by philosophers or pedagogues. It is a problem which confronts us all every single day. Had not the validity of decisions based on conscience always been claimed in daily life, it would never have had to be raised as a significant problem in the first place. This morally pragmatic demand for a universal, intersubjective validity of conscience goes approximately as follows: Anyone who passes a moral judgment based on his conscience thereby makes an unspoken claim that his decision was reached from a neutral standpoint, and that consequently the judgment stands up to rational examination and is based on the formation of conscience. The claim to validity thus also imposes the readiness to expose judgment to rational criticism and, if necessary, to reappraise the workings of conscience.[1]

### THE PRIMACY OF ETHICS

It thus becomes apparent that these practical questions as to the competence of conscience and the claim to validity of judgment are fundamentally ethical questions. They are directed largely towards moral philosophers rather than towards teachers. Hence they should be seen as 'ethically formative' because ethics is fundamentally a system of answers to questions about moral judgments. Its task is to differentiate between moral questions and those which are not; to find satisfactory answers to the former as and when they arise in connection with the moral obligations of the individual; to distinguish his specific needs in reaching decisions and to determine the nature of a complete answer. It is beyond dispute that no theory of education is capable of this. Only ethics is able to determine the formation of conscience and to justify with absolute certainty its judgment as to what is morally right. Hence only an ethical answer can be regarded as satisfactory. Ethics determines how the conscience must proceed if its judgment is to be considered morally justified.

Outside ethics, the problem of the formation of conscience is merely oversimplified and at the same time wrongly interpreted from a pedagogical point of view. Hence it seems to be absolutely essential, with reference to certain ethical insights, to expose any false interpretations of conscience and to establish the validity of an ethical approach. In ethical terms the question as to which approach to the formation of conscience corresponds to contemporary theories of education is not of primary importance. This really is an empirical problem

and can only be solved empirically with the aid of pedagogical knowledge and experience of the structure of psychological motivation, as
well as historical knowledge about the influence of cultural and religious concepts of decisions of conscience. Even when placed on the
empirical level, it is still primarily a philosophical and ethical issue. Its
ethical significance must be analyzed before one can meaningfully use
the experience gained to provide answers to pedagogical questions.
Hence, in the formation of conscience educational methods are subordinate to ethics: that is, the ethical concept of conscience and its methodology.

It must however be admitted that ethics does not facilitate matters
for moral education, which must still choose between the various different concepts of conscience encompassed by ethics. But the understanding of conscience is largely the function of a certain concept of
ethics which is theoretically determined and independent of the actual
practice of ethics. In every approach to ethics a conceptual 'formation
of conscience' takes place in which the theory assumed becomes more
or less fused. It follows that the differing ethical concepts of conscience
are dependent on a given philosophy or theology, although it is agreed
that conscience is a fundamental phenomenon in man and as such represents a universal human existential experience. Conscience and its
function are always seen and examined in connexion with the questions
'What is morality'?, 'What is man'? with their theoretically determined
answers.

## THE ROLE OF CONSCIENCE IN ETHICS

The question then inevitably arises of the precise relationship between the concept of conscience and ethics. This clearly was not a
problem in the structure of traditional moral theology, as can be seen
from the fact that conscience formed a greater part of 'morality in
general' and was subordinate to other themes. As a result of a largely
nominalistic concept of the law it has been reduced to a mere logical
function. It is nothing more than the syllogistic application of the general law to the individual case, its subjective realization. Its place in the
structure of ethics indicates that, in methodological terms, the problem
of conscience presupposes a certain anthropology and theory of law
and is reduced to this. The meaning of conscience within ethics is
methodologically dependent of and determined by these theories.

This brings us to the problem of the conception of ethics and its
autonomy. The traditional conception becomes debatable if we have to
accept that moral duty, expressed in the judgment of conscience, is
determined by the act of the appropriate authority or as the means to

an end for the subject of the action. For this means that ethics is inherently and methodologically dependent on a theory of authority or law and the theory of the ultimate destiny of mankind cannot be autonomous.[2]

Hence the moral philosopher's first task does not consist in examining the structure of human existence—as was too nearly the case with traditional moral theology—but rather, in placing the emphasis on the order of obligation. It all depends on establishing the correct approach to the problem of conscience from which to build up a system of ethics as a theory of moral obligation, and to reach conclusions about its methodological conception. It should not be overlooked that ethics may contribute to a narrowing down of the concept of conscience in that it limits it to a specific function. In so doing, it in effect simplifies moral reality itself. Contemporary ethics, which can no longer ignore Kant's justified principle of autonomy, prohibits us from seeking the precise origins of morality and hence the absolute claim of the moral imperative which manifests itself unequivocally in the conscience. To a certain extent the phenomenon of conscience forms the necessary starting-point for a system of ethics. If moral obligation reveals itself directly through the experience of conscience to be an unequivocal, self-evident phenomenon it must logically be grasped as such and placed at the beginning of any ethical investigation. To place the issue of conscience at the roots of ethics should not, however, lead to any confusion with (moral) psychology. In other words, moral obligation as the initial objective of ethics should not be confused with awareness of obligation or cognizance of responsibility which is the main objective of psychology. But we must differentiate at this point between the act itself and its object; between moral obligation as a moral factor (to the object) and the awareness of obligation as a psychological factor (the act). It must be made clear that these are different questions which cannot logically be equated, and therefore obviously require different answers: to what does morality refer (denotation) and what does morality declare (connotation). Various different designations of 'morality', i.e., morality in the wider sense, can constitute the object of ethics: moral consciousness, awareness of obligation and values; in other words, conscience as a psychological phenomenon. These are certainly ethically relevant aspects for research, but they do not constitute the real core of ethics. Hence we must not drift away from the heart of the problem. The real question of ethics refers to morality as such and its aim is to clarify and define this moral obligation. This is linked with the opinion that if this is its aim, it can be described as morality of conscience. However, from the point of view of the object it is epistemologically autonomous and consequently methodologically independent of any psychological theory of conscience. Any specifically ethical understanding of conscience must take this factor seriously and regard it as a prerequisite for the formation of conscience. In the form of morality of conscience, ethics thus determines the formation of conscience which is the aim of all moral education. It follows that theological ethics cannot proceed in any other way if it wishes to maintain its biblically derived moral code. Moral theology is also a morality of conscience in that it defines conscience as an indispensable hermeneutical principle towards the understanding of ethical tenets of revelation. It is in fact a kind of fore-knowledge analogous to anticipation of the knowledge of revelation.

## THE ACT OF CONSCIENCE: MORAL JUDGMENT

The fact that the conception of ethics is determined by a morality which, through its specifically ethical functions provides the fundamental opportunities for its fulfilment, makes it imperative that we examine the act of conscience itself in closer detail. This justifies the exclusion of certain interpretations of morality and conscience. Nothing is more explicitly stated by moral experience than the fact that it is an essential function of the conscience to pass judgment. Hence it reaches spontaneous judgments or decisions which are guaranteed by conceptual reflection and as a result lead to the establishment of a norm. In this way the conscience assumes an actively creative function. However, this poses the question as to the nature of its judgment, by means of which moral judgments differ from those which are not. It is precisely the task of ethics to establish which elements constitute the structure of a moral judgment.

Elementary moral experience tells us that a judgment fulfils the necessary moral stipulations if it fuses a trans-subjective and an inter-subjective factor: that is, if it possesses an object-subject structure. It gives expression to what is moral as being the obligation of an individual subject and simultaneously the obligation of an individual object, as 'that which is the rightful due'. Only in this way can we define explicitly what we already know and recognize through moral experience; namely, that the moral judgment is directed in towards the subject as well as outwardly towards the object. There is basically no conflict between these subjective and objective functions of moral judgment; rather, they complement each other. On the one hand the subjective definition of the subject and on the other, the objective function of the conscience as an act of informative recognition of the object as the reason for this definition. The moral judgment is thus intrinsic and at the same time established by the object and then translated into a reality by means of its autonomy and the definition of acts.

## CONSEQUENCES FOR THE FORMATION OF CONSCIENCE

An ethically analogous formation of conscience must pay strict attention to this subjective-objective structure of moral judgment in its constitutive and functional aspect. If this is not done, the ensuing disjunction in the form of a mutually opposed play-off and a centrifugal polarization of both functions inevitably leads to the distortion and debasement of the judgment of conscience as a moral judgment.

The first approach, according to which moral judgments must be intrasubjective, goes as follows: a judgment of conscience constitutes a moral judgment when it stems from the subject himself and is an autonomous, free act, his positive definition. For the subject it then becomes the only indispensable instance, informing him of his obligations and thereby causing him to comply with its directives. Only the personal judgment, that is, the personally recognized and acknowledged obligation can be morally binding. The subject is only bound to act morally by means of the affirmation of obligation expressed in the act of judgment. And the subject's autonomy is respected in the formation of conscience. The ethical consequence of this is obvious. It affects above all the heteronomy of a voluntary, that is, morally positivistic ethic, thus contradicting what has been stated so far. On the other hand, it also affects the autonomy (in the Kantian sense) which necessarily has the appearance of a misinterpretation or subjective limitation of the judgment of conscience. On this basis it would not be possible to establish an orthodox formation of conscience.

This intrasubjective function of the moral judgment is by no means a secondary function, but rather a decisive element in moral obligation. This aspect of conscience should on no account be denied; nevertheless, it is not everything. For the conscience also represents the ability of the subject to transcend himself, its judgment causing the subject to turn towards his object and reason for obligation. Without such a connexion the moral judgment would not be a judgment at all! And this leads us to the second aspect, according to which a moral judgment must be trans-subjective at the same time: that it be directed towards the object, towards reality. The individual concerned is subject to the moral judgment not only because it is his own, but also to a greater extent because it is a judgment in the first place, an act of recognition about what in fact objectively commits us. Moral obligation is never more than a given aspect of the individual judgment, yet it transcends the actual process of judging and is aimed towards its object. It commits us as a judgment in so far as it is true and objectively correct. It is thus part of the nature of conscience that we not only remain true to our judgment and that it simultaneously characterizes an openness towards the truth. The criterion of the objective claim to validity, that the judgment is either true or false does not depend on the subject's powers of conviction, but rather on the object of the issue to be realized. This binding object about which the subject passes a judgment and to which it gives 'itself' as manifested in elementary moral experience, is the human dignity of the individual. To be more precise, through his humanity, the individual's personal existence assumes a dignity which is exposed to observation through his behaviour. The individual is thus the object and reason behind the subject's objective moral judgment, thereby expressing his recognition and affirmation as an integral human being.[3]

This aspect of the moral judgment as an act of conscience also requires the appropriate formation of conscience which must in turn be aware of the obvious danger of a disintegration of moral judgment. This occurs in the first instance when insufficient emphasis is laid upon the intrasubjective function as a result of which the objective is stressed to such an extent that it leads to objective extremism. In this way the creative force of the subject's freedom and the limiting function of his conscience are totally excluded. By means of this shift of emphasis and the ensuing false principle of autonomy of absolute freedom, this explicit rejection of the objective purpose of moral obligation is equivalent to a destruction of the moral judgment and makes any formation of conscience educationally dangerous.

The consequences for the formation of conscience of a split in the integrally structured moral judgment and hence an extremely subjective or objective reduction in ethics manifest themselves plainly in the image of man on which it is based. For the image of man arising from moral experience is not in the least arbitrary; on the contrary, it is a perception of mankind which corresponds to that implied in the moral obligation. It must correspond to the moral facts. The image presupposed by ethics is the result of reflection as to the meaning of man based on the moral facts.[4] According to experience man, as both subject and object, must fulfil all possible conditions of the moral facts if he is to appear as subject and object. Given that he factually appears as such, he possesses a specific anthropological 'physiognomy'. One can clearly discern a thinking, autonomous being capable of finding, justifying and fulfilling the ethical norm. The moral facts thus imply that the sole reason for their existence is the truth about mankind and how this should be recognized by those wishing to come to terms with the indisputable fact of moral actions. This reductive link between moral obligation and human existence and, in accordance with ethics, anthropology, is not an attempt to find a metaphysical 'derivation' for morality. On the contrary, without succumbing to a naturalistic paralogism, it is nevertheless possible to localize the task of conscience formation in the face of this anthropological background. For any system of ethics in which the anthropological aspects are not correct can only have a superficial effect on the formation of conscience. Hence we can thus state clearly that the formation of conscience must remain closely linked to ethics as the theory of morality, and this by extension implies that this demand coincides with an anthropological outlook. From this starting point further insights into the nature of man are gained: in the moral sphere is man a homo creator or a homo contemplator? The exclusive division on the epistemological level into subject and object leads to the alternation of activity and passivity and is finally resolved on the ontological level into the mutual opposition of man and world (man and objects), and man and God. As implied earlier, this has ethical consequences for the formation of conscience, in that when the subject is given absolute autonomy it results in creativity, as for example in German idealism, in Marxism and in existentialism. Its influence over the creation of values and norms is also apparent in contemporary moral theology. On the other hand when the object is given absolute autonomy this gives rise to a passively receptive contemplativeness derived from essentialism or substantialism in materialistic (nineteenth-century mechanistic materialism, Freudianism and behaviourism) or metaphysical form (certain interpretations of Neo-Thomism, the doctrine of natural law, as well as from the biblical positivism of revelation). A dialectical position also found in Marxism, which attempts to overcome the rift between subject and object, manifests itself clearly in the moral theological debate about natural law.[5] From this insight we can easily draw consequences relevant to the formation of conscience.

*Translated by Sarah Twohig*

## Notes

1. N. Hoerster, *Ethik und Moral: Texte zur Ethik*, ed. D. Birnbacher and N. Hoerster (Munich, 1976), pp. 17–22.

2. T. Styczen, '*Autonomie und christliche Ethik als methodologisches Problem*' in *Theol. u. Glaube* 66 (1976), pp. 211–9.

3. T. Styczen, 'W sprawie etyki niezalezne j' in *Roczniki Filozoficzne* 24 (1976), vol. 2.

4. Noteworthy in this respect are the attempts of the Polish philosophers R. Ingarden, *Über die Verantwortung. Ihre ontische Fundamente* (Stuttgart, 1970) and Cardinal K. Wojtyla, *Osoba i czyn* [Man and Action] (Cracow, 1969).

5. F. Böckle, *Das Naturrecht im Disput* (Düsseldorf, 1966); *Naturrecht in der Kritik*, ed. F. Böckle and E.-W. Böckenförde (Mainz, 1973).

Alfons Auer

# Christianity's Dilemma: Freedom to Be Autonomous or Freedom to Obey?

IN THE modern history of freedom the incompatibility of autonomy and obedience has become widely accepted as a kind of dogma. The place held by authority and obedience in Christianity seems to confirm this dogma. Obedient subjection to the will of God is a central point in the revealed religion of the Old and New Testaments. It is true that the New Testament puts authority and obedience under the overriding concept of God's self-revealing love. For a long time the representatives of the Church's authority saw themselves, like the apostles, as Christ's co-workers, and explained their 'higher position' as a charismatic call to loving and humble service. In order to break the identification of the Church with the political system which had become increasingly tighter since Constantine, Gregory VII demanded a 'fully autonomous and independent system of laws' for the spiritual community of the Church and the basis of this system should be the overriding authority of the papacy over the Church and the political State. Since the Council of Trent this grew into a more and more effective 'mysticism of authority' which was marked by 'the idea of a complete identification of God's will with the institutional expression of authority'.[1] In the general condition of the moral orientation of life, in which not everybody can easily understand all that is implied, there was less concern about giving people an insight in the inherent value of what was commanded and in that way evoking 'obedience' than about creating the readiness to obey the authority which claimed a divine mandate. And when 'freedom to obey' remains fixed in that kind of context, there is an unsolvable dilemma between it and the 'freedom to be autonomous'.

## THE SUPPOSED DILEMMA

A closer look shows the modern assertion that autonomy and obedience cannot be reconciled to be for a large part a mere assumption. Freedom, autonomy and obedience are in principle quite compatible.

1. *Autonomy implies obedience.* For Kant—though not for all who refer to him—freedom to be autonomous is not freedom to do as one likes but a freedom which man only becomes aware of when faced by moral law and which puts him under the law. The controversial explosiveness of the concept of autonomy lies in the rejection of 'being immature through one's own fault'. Kant demands that man 'be only subject to his own and nevertheless universal code of laws'.[2] He who is responsible for himself must also affirm his determination through his natural and personal environment. The acceptance of the freedom of one's own existence also means the acceptance of the free existence of everybody else. For this entire determining law Kant demands 'respect'. But does this 'respect for the law' not come very close to 'obedience'?—Where, then, is the dilemma?

2. *Obedience tends towards autonomy.* Just as autonomy cannot be separated from obedience and duty, so must obedience and duty be interpreted in view of autonomy. Obedience without understanding and a will of one's own would only be a blind and slavish obedience, and therefore unworthy of man. 'Man is only obedient when, with full understanding of the law, he makes it the law of his own will, but this means that he gives himself this law'.[3] In obedience man fulfils the unspecified claim of his own existence, as it emerges in his moral awareness; he verifies the fact that he is committed to the rationality of reality. Obedience therefore tends towards the optimal performance of autonomy. So, once again: where is the dilemma?

3. *Freedom makes autonomy and obedience possible.* Freedom is not just the ability to choose here this and there that. In freedom man is entrusted with his own self as potential and as demand. It is in freedom that he has to answer for his own autonomy. And just as freedom is the foundation of autonomy, so it is the foundation of obedience. In freedom man also affirms 'the other freedom', which demands to be recognized by him ('Respect for the law', 'obedience'). The concept of freedom is a matter of communication: 'Man alone by himself cannot be free . . . The intercourse of freedom comes transcendentally before the subject, and the concept of the subject already contains the transcendentally and logically preceding concept of inter-subjectivity'.[4] Once more: where is the dilemma? When the interrelationship is seen like this, the notions of freedom, autonomy and obedience come so close to each other that they become almost interchangeable. But it is

said that the widespread factual deformation of obedience as 'heteronomous' obedience makes the concept almost unusable, even in the context of the formula of 'rational obedience' (E. Fromm). And yet, the ideas of freedom and autonomy move nonetheless in a kind of twilight. When all three concepts are interpreted in an equally authentic way, one can in any case not see any dilemma between them. Frankly, the more we concern ourselves actually with reality, the less we can avoid this conclusion.

## THE TRUE DILEMMA

1. *The dilemma comes to the fore when autonomy and obedience are misunderstood.* Misunderstanding arises when autonomy is interpreted as opposed to any dependence and orientation, as the absence of a 'universal code of laws', and when obedience is seen as blind subjection to some 'irrational authority' or as refusing to take upon oneself one's own responsibility for oneself. In both cases there is a misunderstanding since there is no autonomy without 'respect for the law' and there is no true obedience without understanding of what is commanded or at least of the competence of the commanding authority. Both kinds of misunderstanding are part and parcel of the reality of everyday human life but can in principle be avoided.

2. *The dilemma becomes inevitable in so far as the tension between one's own and other people's freedom has become historically and factually inevitable.* The one area, common to all, where freedom can become a reality is limited. Within the context of the 'intercourse of freedom' every freedom of one's own limits the freedom of others; this diminution of freedom must be accepted by all. But the experience of these limitations constantly gives rise to vital impulses which try to achieve a more acceptable and less unreasonable division of the area of freedom which we share in common. Yet, 'an absolutely factual totally *free* consensus of the concrete division of an area of freedom, based on principles or conditioned by the age . . . among all those entitled to freedom will never be adequately worked out'.[5] There will always be new situations which imply the coercion of a decision. The moment of coercion cannot be eliminated from the intercourse of freedom.

3. *The dilemma becomes most acute when authority establishes for itself the right and duty to restrict the autonomy which one individual or all strive to achieve by making unreasonable demands on their obedience and by forcing them through the use of power when they refuse.* Over against the claim of each one's own freedom the authority must explain and pursue the claim of the other freedoms. In so far as an authority is serious about the *function of interpretation,* that is, the channelling and

concrete interpretation of 'the legal force of the universal will',[6] and shows itself competent to do so, it proves itself to be a 'rational authority' in Fromm's sense. Only sensible reasoning can set the process of persuasion going. The command must be made intelligible by explaining its purpose. '[But] aims must be kept in view until they have been reached. If we may carry this image further—the norm must be steered towards the aim; it will hit the target, not logically, but only teleologically. This is why the presentation of the aim is decisive for actions that apply the norm [and explain the norm—Author] as these presentations are linked with the norm as the standard for such regulations—their so-called "ratio" '.[7] In any case, authority has to legitimate itself with arguments. It may fail on this point either because its claim does not rest on a sufficiently mature 'respect for the law' or because it thinks it can dispense with the trouble of trying to argue things out sensibly or also because some concrete norm can no longer convincingly express the claim of freedom with regard to moral experience.

Yet, this kind of thing drives the dilemma to its most acute point. For, apart from interpretation, the authority also has the *task to carry out* 'the legal force of the universal will'. It has to achieve in a concrete historical way precisely that which it sees as the minimum of order in the common weal of the community which it has to protect. The hope to achieve some consensus of all on the basis of voluntary acceptance truly belongs to the permanent stock of the great utopias of mankind. But the authority cannot indefinitely postpone its protection of threatened freedom and has to meet the individual's here-and-now refusal to 'respect' the universal law. This task is taken over by the criminal law by means of threats and the application of external sanctions. The ethical demand carries its sanction in itself: the historical experience of life sooner or later provides the existential check-test of the right or wrong use of freedom. Nevertheless, neither educational nor social authority can wash its hands of the use of coercive means in order to ensure a minimum of social order in freedom by relying on those sanctions of ethical demands in general. In so far as those concerned yield to sheer force there can frankly be no talk of moral obedience. But moral obedience can and must be generated by the fact that authority shows itself in the end determined and patient—a 'rational authority'. The criteria for this legitimation can here only be listed, not developed in detail. (*a*) Even when an authority has to use coercive means it must not forego the attempt to show the plausibility of its demands as well as possible. (*b*) When an educational authority has to enforce demands or orders this can only be done usefully in an atmosphere of love and personal credibility. The spontaneous moral response of a child or an adolescent cannot be evoked by orders but only through love, and, apart from this, the ordering of life, pressed forward in education, must become tangible and humanly attractive in the educator's example as a symbol.[8] (c) The use of force must also be shown to be such that the insight into the historical nature of the forms of human achievements is not confused by apodictic and absolute generalizations of a past style of life and remains open and alert to the 'signs of the time'. Rebelliousness can indicate a lack of 'respect for the law', but it is often also the expression of the experience that a law which is still valid and actually insisted upon limps along behind an already developing demand which will only later find its full legitimation. (d) The objective which is the measure of any demand for obedience must be the unfolding of autonomy and not hold people down in a state of immaturity. The reason pursued by the authority must one day be seen by the person now still under obedience as his own reason and accepted as such. This is why he who gives the order must deliberately envisage the liberation of him who obeys so that he can genuinely be responsible for himself.

CHRISTIANITY CONFRONTED BY THE DILEMMA: FREEDOM TO BE
AUTONOMOUS OR FREEDOM TO OBEY?

The question now arises whether the specific nature of God on which Christian moral education bases its claim implies definite consequences with regard to the dilemma set out here. An answer to this problem will be proposed in what follows in two theses: in so far as Christian teaching and practice bring to bear an authoritarian image of God we meet with a drastic bar to the idea of freedom to be autonomous and a massive clinging to the ideology of a narrow obedience. But in so far as preaching brings out a God of creative love and freedom, Christianity can and must face the dilemma of autonomy and obedience.

1. *Christian obstruction of autonomy.* In more recent history there has been a considerable expansion of the area of freedom for human autonomy. This is the historical outcome of scientific-technological and socially emancipating processes which have become decisive for the lines on which modern man has developed. From the start this freedom movement has been frowned upon by the Christian churches. Above all the Catholic Church has tried time and again to oppose these trends towards freedom by demanding of the faithful a definite readiness to obey the Church's leadership based on God's mandate. It preferred to forego its effective presence in modern society and claimed itself to be the *societas perfecta* rather than to risk itself by getting mixed up with the freedom movements of this modern age. During the last century Church leaders as well as theologians and Catholic philosophers deci-

sively rejected the idea of autonomy. Even today many theologians and Catholic thinkers hold that autonomy and theonomy are incompatible and judge that the attempt to show compatibility between moral autonomy and religious obedience is a subversion of the substance of the Christian ethos into a flat so-called enlightened morality, and even a sell-out of all that is Christian. Nobody, surely, can fail to see the misinterpretations of autonomy in theory and practice. On the basis of such misinterpretations it is impossible to have intelligent discussions; one can only contribute to the increasing fixation of the pseudo-dilemma between autonomy and obedience and by the same token make the Christian opposition to freedom more acute.

2. *The Christian orientation towards freedom to be autonomous and to obey.* The built-in consequences through which the Christian understanding of God reveals the apparent aspect of the dilemma and the ways to overcome the real dilemma between autonomy and obedience can be shown in three statements.

(a) *The mystery of creation implies laying the foundation of freedom.* 'Creation' does not mean the production of a ready-made world but establishing its initial shape and the inauguration of its history. As 'God's likeness' (Gen. 1:27) man is called upon to activate the potential built into the initial shape. When Thomas Aquinas introduces his *Ethics* in the prologue to Part II of his *Summa Theologica* he brings up the concept of 'being like unto God': man is God's image in so far as he is the 'principle of his deeds' and has 'a free will and power over his actions'. Here Thomas speaks as a theologian about man's autonomy: man is principle of his self, master of his deeds, cause of his self, he is 'his own law' (Romans 2:14). He lets the traditional presentation of God's majesty and sovereignty (*ipsum esse, ipsa forma, causa prima, providentia universalis*) culminate and prove itself in the thesis that God 'puts his creatures so far outside himself and leaves them so much to their independence that they not only have an existence of their own but also their own causality . . . to the point of their own direction across one another, . . . to the point of the freedom to be "a kind of cause of his own self" '.[9] The concept of God's image shows in fact how the transcendent and the immanent aspects of man's destiny flow into each other; in man this being geared to the original Image and the imitating this original Image meet in a fulfilled human existence, in freedom to obey and freedom to be autonomous. In this obedient working out of his being geared to God man experiences the courage to be himself.

(b) *The mystery of sin implies a warning about freedom.* Both autonomy and obedience are constantly in danger of degenerating. As in the course of his history man succumbed to this danger he set himself against the divine will concerning this world. Thomas Aquinas stressed precisely this anthropological dimension of sin when he wrote: 'God is only offended by us because we act against our own well-being'.[10] Autonomy is perverted when self-rule is understood in such a way that there is no room for its foundation in God nor for its being geared to the universal law (autonomism and libertinism). Obedience is perverted when man seeks salvation in the fulfilment of external legal regulations or refuses to accept responsibility for himself (legalism and infantilism).[11]

The warning does not only hold for the individual but also for the Church's leadership. The Church disregards both autonomy and obedience when it asserts some competence which is not clearly enough founded either in itself or with regard to the concrete subject-matter and for which nevertheless blind obedience is demanded. But neither does the Church take the 'warning about freedom' seriously when it does not fulfil its critical function with regard to man's freedom to be autonomous, when it lacks the courage to put forward rationally based patterns of social order in the general moral debate to counter destructive tendencies in contemporary awareness or when, faced with the increasingly public and obvious ambivalence of technological and social attempts to manipulate people, it hides behind naiveté or lack of competence.

(c) *The mystery of salvation implies the eschatological liberation which leads to freedom.* The God proclaimed by Jesus is anything but 'authoritarian'. In the historical development of his teaching 'authoritarian' elements have only too often blocked the view of the Father of Jesus Christ. The parable of the prodigal son shows an apparently 'permissive' father: he does not try to save the son from misery by force; he relies on love and its power to inspire freedom, and he proves right in the end. In his behaviour towards the son who stayed at home he also relies on freedom and persuasion. He does not force him to come to the feast; he goes out to him and 'entreats him' (Lk. 15). The meeting with the young man also shows that Jesus imposes no freedom on anybody, nor does he manipulate anybody into freedom if he wants to remain unfree. But in his appeal to man he puts man before a decisive choice and with his love he tries to entice him to take the path of freedom (Mt. 19). In Jesus the God of love turns to the sick and the sinner, the poor and the outcast, and eats with them. The understanding of God's sovereignty as the sovereignty of love is concentrated in the fact that Jesus speaks of God as his and our Father. The description of God as 'Father' occurs 170 times in the gospels—impressive evidence for the fundamental belief that through Jesus God is close to man in love. What is special about Jesus' kind of love is precisely that it is motivated by its being turned towards man. The fellowship taught and lived by Jesus is rooted in the Father's love and draws from this its measure, its direction and its inner freedom. It is not just a matter of humanity, but of making God's love present among men and of man's salvation.

Just as Jesus offered freedom to all men through his love, so his followers should create freedom and maturity. Jesus' message of freedom and love, when taken seriously, creates without any doubt a new moral climate and inspires a new style of moral grounding which can meet the positive spiritual tendencies of our age in a more fruitful way than nervous conservatism, legalistic security-seeking and self-chosen ghetto situations through a mystified obedience and sterile mistrust of man's determination to answer for himself.[12] Theonomy, thankfulness for man's existence, obedient submission to God's will and acceptance of divine forgiveness, all this is for the uncompromising humanist always still the more or less sublimated terminology of an authoritarian irrationalism. But for Christians it is the terminology of the true autonomy and the true obedience of a liberated way of being human. Only the historical effectiveness of their faith can convincingly show that in this fundamental area the dilemma between autonomy and obedience is but a supposed one. But where, however, the dilemma is insoluble and a fact of constantly painful experience Christians have to show in a credible way that it becomes bearable and even can contribute to the freedom to be autonomous and obedient at a higher level when it is coped with in the perspective of that love through which Jesus enables us to take charge of our own life in an obedient, yet responsible way and humbly to accept also the incompatible situations which arise along with it.

## Notes

1. Yves Congar, *Problems of Authority* (London, 1961).

2. H. Vorländer (ed.), *Grundlegung zur Metaphysik der Sitten* (Der philosophischen Bibliothek, vol. 41, Hamburg, 1957), p. 56; cf. pp. 42–65 and pp. 71 f.

3. J. Schwartländer, *Der Mensch ist Person. Kants Lehre vom Menschen* (Stuttgart-Berlin-Cologne-Mainz, 1968), p. 165, but see esp. pp. 160–8.

4. H. Krings, 'Freiheit', in *Handbuch philosophischer Grundbegriffe*, ed. by this author, study edition vol. 2 (Munich, 1973), pp. 493–510; for this ref. see p. 507.

5. K. Rahner, *Gnade als Freiheit* [*Grace as Freedom*] (Freiburg, 1968), p. 71.

6. I. Kant, *Grundlegung zur Metaphysik der Sitten*, p. 55.

7. J. Esser, *Vorverständniss und Methodenwahl in der Rechtfindung. Rationalitätsgrundlagen richterlicher Entscheidungspraxis* (Frankfurt, 2nd ed., 1972), p. 34.

8. Cf. authors such as: F. März, 'Gehorsam', in *Lexikon der Pädagogik* (ed. H. Rombach, vol. 2, Freiburg-Basle-Vienna, 1970), p. 82; W. J. Revers, 'Das Gewissen in der Entrfaltung der Persönlichkeit', in *Jahrbuch für Psychologie und Psychotherapie* 6 (1959), pp. 142–53; W. Heinen, *Liebe als sittliche Grundkraft und ihre Fehlformen* (3rd ed., Freiburg, 1968); J. M. Hollenbach, *Der Mensch als Entwurf* (Frankfurt, 1957).

9. E. Przywara, *Crucis Mysterium* (Paderborn, 1939), pp. 67 f: As Thomas brings Aristotelian thought into the traditional sacral world of Dominican and Franciscan Augustinianism, he presses on from 'sacralism' to 'secularism'.

10. *Summa contra Gentiles*, III, 122: 'Non enim Deus a nobis offenditur nisi ex eo quod contra nostrum bonum agimus'.

11. It can of course be a high performance of the freedom to be autonomous when someone renounces the actual disposal of oneself for the sake of higher purposes, as, say, in the case of religious vows.

12. A 'new style of ethical education' is treated in greater detail by A. Auer, in *Die Aktualität der sittlichen Botschaft Jesu: Die Frage nach Jesus* (Graz-Vienna-Cologne, 1973), pp. 271–363, esp. pp. 318–26, where the meaning of Jesus' message with regard to present ethical trends (development of maturity, activation of responsibility for and commitment to the world) is dealt with.

Henri de Lavalette

# Personal Development and Social Involvement

ONE of the distinguishing marks of Christianity, at least in theory, is its rejection of a dilemma that appears often in the history of cultures, philosophies and religions: the choice between personal salvation or happiness, the ultimate in personal development, on the one hand, and, on the other, the primacy of a collective Kingdom we have to build, to which we owe all sacrifices and our entire devotion. The Christian's tragic conflict is not the choice between Creon and Antigone, but that of the martyr who, while testifying to his personal fidelity to the end, dies for the sake of the people by desacralizing politics. In the face of political religion, the Christian witness is to a true religion belonging not to the realm of convention and legalism, but to personal conscience and freedom. Unlike 'elect' or gnostic sects, who shrug off the burden of saving a world they see as evil, the Christian sheds his blood for the sake of future peace and reconciliation. Eschatological hope in a God who is all in all forbids, on principle, destructive choices.

Each age and culture summons Christians, more or less readily, to find practical and theoretical means of rejecting the dilemma. The constitution *Gaudium et Spes* is itself a rejection of the dilemma between personal development and social involvement, a rejection already testified to by generations of militant Christians: no, we will not opt for personal happiness in another world at the expense of practical involvement in this one. No, religion is not the opium of the people.

Yet neither *Gaudium et Spes* nor the post-conciliar 'political theologies' have provided a totally satisfactory theological framework for this double rejection, or defined positive objectives. There are three aspects under which this failure can be seen, and a consideration of them will enable us at least to pose the ethical question in terms suited to our age.

## INDIVIDUAL CONDITIONING BY MODELS AND TRANSFORMATION OF THE MODELS BY INDIVIDUALS

On the most superficial level, the first thing that strikes one is the extraordinary proliferation of societal models. Not only does democracy mean different things if we are talking of a liberal or a popular democracy, but capitalism and socialism are now plurivalent terms, covering the whole spectrum of balance between State control and individual freedom. What can appear as an arbitrary choice in the spread of available possible choices most often in fact turns out to be the product of historical and cultural processes determined by power struggles. Furthermore, sociologists teach us that one society contains ethnic and class sub-cultures, anti-cultures, fringe cultures, and so on.

This is not just a striking illustration of the Tower of Babel, of multiplying a phenomenon of dispersal. It also illustrates, in the interplay of struggle inside each nation and between nations, a capacity for collective and interdependent change.

Accepting this aspect of the contemporary world shows us that the practical form taken by our rejection of the dilemma cannot take exactly the same shape as before. If the recommended Christian attitude of the past can be summed up in one word, that word would be *corrective.* If you were among the well-off in a liberal society, sensitive to the values of personal development, creative personal initiative, etc., well and good, but you should not forget that your personalism should extend to a personalism of the community; you had to put these values within the reach of everyone through service, teaching, and so on. But today we have to accept something that would earlier have seemed contradictory: realizing that the individual and his personal values are far more socially conditioned than was previously thought, and yet not regarding these conditionings as a quasi-natural phenomenon, but as something to be worked on in order to produce a more just society.

## COMMUNITY DISRUPTION AND INDIVIDUAL DEPERSONALIZATION

The second aspect is the appearance of soulless masses and the trampling of the individual underfoot. It has been examined a hundred times, from different but convergent angles. The growing dependence of the individual on centres of the 'decision-making process' in politics, economics and technocracy, centres he can hardly identify; the manufacturing of his needs, even his cultural and leisure needs, by the 'consumer society'; the artificiality of publicity and fashion, and the pseudo-information doled out by the mass-media: all these have been dissected and denounced *ad nauseam*. The sociologists, whether neo-capitalist like Reisman, or neo-Marxist like the Frankfurt school, show the same feeling of helplessness; so do the young of today, far removed from the revolutionary illusions of the late sixties. In the Third World too, taking stock of the deep cultural and social destruc-tion vented on it, and the strength of the bonds holding it in a state of economic dependence on the industrialized nations it can hardly hope to catch up with in the foreseeable future, the same feeling of despair is eroding earlier hopes: the theology of liberation is giving way to a theology of captivity.

And yet personal investigation and communal development are perhaps not contradictory pulls to be equalized so much as unex-pressed forms of the same quest, for a lost 'world' in which society and the individual can each grow through the other's development. Pursuit of 'body awareness' is also awareness of a possible way back to the deepest roots of expression and communication. The new emphasis on ecology is a quest for control of the environment. Political parties, however opposed to each other, latch on to the slogans of participation and self-sufficiency. Society has of course already seized on these new forces and produced new products, new associations, and new public-ity: all new sources of revenue, new ways of providing the illusion of satisfaction and exploiting longings. But the need for these is not purely an artificial one, and the observation still holds good: we are no longer faced with a choice between personal development and social involve-ment, but with two tasks to be undertaken side by side.

Such a state of affairs can bring surprising results. For lack of adequate nourishment, the most varied efforts follow one another in rapid succession, hold the forefront of the stage for a time, and are then as quickly forgotten. Naïvety and scepticism feed on one another, while the constant danger of commercial or ideological exploitation of ideals engenders distrust and rejection. If, in theory, the rooting of theoretical discourse in practice has never been held in such esteem, in fact it is above all the *spectacle* of practice that animates reports and conversations. Society is listening to its own chest. It finds the diag-nosis hard, cannot distinguish its symptoms or decide on its illness: are we in a crisis of cyclical trade depression or is our whole civilization in crisis? If the sickness is new, how do we measure the efficacy of our remedies, and how long should we give them to work? Reports, as well as enquiries, succeed one another at ever decreasing intervals— including reports on evangelization.

## PERSONALIZATION AND COMMUNAL CONSTRUCTION:
### THE SITUATION IN THE CHURCH TODAY

The third aspect concerns us, Christians. Christianity is on principle, as Chesterton said, a whole education in itself. Confessing Christ Jesus is surely learning not to separate the individual Jesus from the community that is his body, and to recognize that what holds his body together is personal relationship with Jesus, in his Spirit? One is not born a Christian, one becomes one; so there can be no substitute for the personal, constantly renewed, decision of faith. But the theological life of the Christian unfolds in the demand and research for a common faith; it is open to the hope of the Kingdom, and expressed in effective and inventive acts of love for one's neighbour, for his own sake and in all dimensions of his being, corporal as well as spiritual, collective as well as individual.

The overtures and hopes stemming from the Second Vatican Council must be recognized. By re-defining the concept of the local or individual Church, and giving it a position of fundamental importance, the Council was reacting against a menacing and depersonalizing alignment of the Church on the side of technocratic and bureaucratic government. It was showing the need to combine a feeling and respect for *differences* with a genuine quest for and manifestation of *communion*. Personalization and communal involvement were seen as needs and tasks of equally growing importance. And the Council was well aware that this *aggiornamento,* while based on theology, was no less responsive to the needs and tasks of secular society, as it showed by its insistence on the 'principle of subsidiarity'.

The Council, however, left many of its tasks unfinished, both on the practical level, such as a constitution of the rights of individual Churches, and in its pursuit of revisions of theory, particularly in the field of ethics. In the social and political spheres, the Church was increasingly tending to renounce its claim to define its own 'social teaching' and to relate itself to States as one power to another, through Concordats; it was inviting Christians to let their own political judgment be formed by the requirements of the Gospel seen in the light of particular situations brought about by history, culture, appertaining to such-and-such a political regime or social class. The key word was to become 'legitimate pluralism', pluralism legitimized by the impossibility of defining a political view applicable as of right to all situations and all values.

But this pluralism was not extended to family life and sexuality: here the socio-cultural conditioning of personal behaviour was only taken into account in pastoral application of principles. Moral teaching is still

presented as 'normative', as defining something universally and objectively good or bad, because supposedly based on 'nature', on human
biology for example. While the Council itself was still using the lan-
guage of 'natural law' in the social and political spheres, and left
sexual morality on the question of contraception open to future revision
by the Pope, the post-Conciliar period has seen a reinforcement of the
dual standard of moral teaching already in evidence before the
Council—with the critical results we all know. Within the Church,
there would now be two opposing parties, arguing one *against* the
other, either for the primacy of the 'official' morality of the Church-
institution, or for that of the individual believing conscience. The ac-
cusations levelled against the hierarchy in this respect can in some
senses be seen as contradictory: those who object to its authoritarianism in matters of family morality accuse it of not taking a firm
enough stand on political matters. The hierarchy claims a prophetic
resistance to the weight of public opinion, while its critics claim a
prophetic evangelism in protesting against the extrinsicalist legalism of
the teaching Church. A paralysis is taking hold of the Church: the
hierarchy is vainly multiplying its appeals for obedience and modera-
tion; fewer and fewer people are listening, and it knows it. But then
what weight do the protests and fringe or temporary groupings of its
opponents carry? It is ridiculous and suicidal to try to seize power in
the Church by force, so they are reduced to ineffective discussions, and
they know it. Both sides suffer from the same sense of impotence,
echoing that reigning in secular society.

### BEYOND THE MENACE OF FALSE DILEMMAS

A frank recognition of the existence of this state of affairs is the first
prerequisite for avoiding the false choices often put forward: as Christians, should we first seek to be saints, since history teaches us that no
deep reform in the Church can come from 'above', worked out on the
basis of elaborate institutional reforms; or should we work for a change
of structures, if it is true that our age feels the conditioning weight of
structures as never before? By presenting us with poster images, 'they'
force us to choose between being Francis of Assisi—who, when he
heard a mysterious call to rebuild 'my Father's house', never dreamt of
trying to reform the Church, but only naively of restoring a ruined
chapel—or Camilo Torres, for whom the call meant a call to arms as a
revolutionary. But this is forgetting that Francis, through his rediscov-
ery of the evangelical call to poverty, could not help coming into conflict with the rich, established Church of the Middle Ages, and that
Camilo Torres committed himself to the cause of the oppressed in order
to resolve the personal dilemma of finding himself a priest of a Church

bound to its colonial past: rightly or wrongly, it was the impossibility of living this personal hypocrisy that led him to make the final break. In fact, the only 'first' we are obliged to seek is the Kingdom of God. And the Kingdom is above the false opposition between common good and individual good.

Perhaps a new wisdom is taking shape in the apparent paralysis of the Church, a wisdom that looks beyond slogans and recipes. Teaching is not enough. Vatican II provided the teaching. It was a useful teaching in that it corrected false representations inherited from the past. While classical theology tended to oppose (through distinguishing them) 'virtues' (for personal spiritual growth) and 'charisms' (gifts for the use of the social body of the Church), the Council helped to bring together the two meanings of the Christian term *edificatio:* the meaning of 'building-up' the Body of the Church through charisms, the highest of which produce faith, hope and charity, and that of 'edification' in the monastic and ascetic sense to which later spiritual writings had restricted it. It also denied the existence of a dual Christian morality: the maximalist, witnessing morality of 'counsels', and the minimalist one of 'precepts', confined to observation of the Law. Finally, the Council forcefully reaffirmed that the Church finds its justification not in itself but in its mission.

If this teaching is not to remain an ideological mask, practice must be made to correspond to it—on all levels. There are certainly some institutional reforms needed: when will Canon Law apply the principle of subsidiarity in the Latin Roman Church? When will the individual Church cease to be a concept and become a reality? But the institutional framework will still be an empty shell if Christians cannot redevelop the sense of and taste for *wisdom,* in its most traditional applications. Wisdom does not stem from a closed anthropology: allowing 'negative anthropology' a large part, it leaves room for group experience (popular wisdom, political wisdom, national wisdom) and individual experience (individual intuitions, the expertise of those recognized as wise). Without denying the irreducibility of personal decision, it is shaped in communication and exchange. It is based on tradition, history and practice, yet is critical and does not hesitate to challenge cultural pseudo-evidence. It neither dictates a code nor utters prophetic cries, but works away at building a life-style and a community project. It does not oppose sociology and psychology, what can be worked out and what is to be hoped for, the subjective and the objective. It is not moralizing. It is the principle of growth before God and man, the ally of the Kingdom.

*Translated by Paul Burns*

Jacques-Marie Pohier

# Preaching on the Mountain or Dining with Whores?

PROFESSORS of ethics or those responsible for moral education are rarely sentenced to death for immorality by the civil or religious authorities of their time. Much more often they more or less consciously aid and abet those in power and the interests of the various 'orders'. And those in power would not hesitate, like Napoleon, to invent God if he did not exist, for God is very useful for keeping ordinary people on the right road. Fortunately, whatever there is in morals—when it is there at all—that has been invented by and for man, is not the product of teachers of morality or ethical experts. It is the product of men who, in order to be such human geniuses or moral or holy men, geniuses of the human or divine order, have had to locate themselves beyond the level of what our ordinary common wisdom is obliged to say in the paradoxes and contradictions that it cannot surmount, often while honouring far too inadequately whichever one of the two terms which it suggests are contradictory. But it pays far too high a price in order to escape from these dilemmas with which it marks out the everyday ways of men. Even when it rewards the priests and teachers of morals who bow down before its demands, it kills the Socrateses, the Jesuses of Nazareth and others in other civilizations and in other ages.

When Christians ask themselves in what way Christian moral training is original, they should not forget that Jesus was not the only man condemned for blasphemy and immorality by the religious and civil authorities of his time. Others had to give their lives so that their message could bear fruit. But Christians may rest assured that their way of contributing to more education is only fit to be called Christian if they behave in a way that is as socially and religiously scandalous as the behaviour of Jesus Christ on the one hand in dining with whores, on the other in his sermon on the mount, and if they do that for one reason and one reason only: and that reason, now as in the past, is even more scandalous than the things done.

### MORAL EDUCATION IN PREACHING ON THE MOUNTAIN

Even if Jesus probably did not actually give the sermon on the mount, (which it is quite tenable to say is a posthumous collection of teachings, a good number of which were spoken by Jesus himself), Jesus did teach morals. After twenty centuries of Christianity, we find it rather difficult to realize to what extent that teaching was both blasphemous and immoral, both in content and in form. In form: ' "You have heard that it was said to the men of old . . . But I say to you . . ." ' (Mt. 5:21–2 et seq.). In content: in ascribing authority to himself Jesus offers qualifications of the Law, and in this particular instance modifications of morality. The daring of form and content are one and the same. There is no parallel in ancient Judaism to these antithetical formulas of Jesus: no doctor of the law, no scribe, no rabbi, no professor of justice has dared to say after presenting the Law ('You heard that it was said to the men of old . . .'): 'But I say to you'; because no one had in terms of content dared to do what Jesus did: namely, to touch the Law.

Even more disturbing is the fact that Jesus does not always refer to the Law in the same way. If he had always corrected it in a wider sense, he could have passed for lax and impious, and could have been easily avoided as such. If he had always corrected it in a more severe way, he could have passed for a fanatic and could no less easily have been shunned as such. But he modified the Torah both in a wider and in a more exacting way. In fact mere interference with the Torah was enough to make an immoral blasphemer. He radicalized it in regard to 'Thou shalt not kill' (Mt. 5:27). He criticized it by categorizing what it said, keeping certain elements but retaining others that the Torah nevertheless associated with the first (for instance, in regard to eschatological vengeance against the heathen in Mt. 11:5–6 and Lk. 4:16–30). He rescinded the Torah: on divorce (Mt. 5:31–2), on oaths (5:33–7), on retaliation (5:38–42).

The sermon on the mount is a tissue of violations of the Law and therefore of morals. What any good Jew might think of that is well brought out in the Tannaitic statement: 'Even of anyone who says only: "(all) the Torah is of God with the exception of this or that verse pronounced not by God but by Moses from his own lips", one may say that he has slandered the word of Yahweh'.[1] In fact the most immoral and blasphemous aspect of Jesus was his pretension to be in himself the accomplishment of the Law: he comes not to abolish it but to fulfil it (Mt. 5:17). The blasphemy in this is that Jesus makes himself equal to God, which is immoral for it means putting oneself above the Law not by escaping from it but in making oneself its creator. This man had to die. He did die for that.

But surely he died too surely. What Jesus did in terms of moral revolution surely died with him altogether. And what rose with him was only a new Torah, henceforth forever congealed above history, just as the resurrected Jesus was to be hypostatized as Christ and Lord, beyond history while waiting for history to be dissolved into his parousia. If that were the case the history of Christian morality would consist in commenting on, discussing, interpreting and elucidating this new Law, this New Testament, this new ethics. That would be the function of all magisteria. But, on the one hand, that is to forget that Jesus much more radically contested the magisterium which elucidated the Torah: the *halakah*, in a way which—like his attitude to the Torah—has no parallel in ancient Judaism.

Above all, if that were the case, we would have forgotten that to be a disciple of Jesus Christ does not consist in repeating him but in imitating him. It is not a question of refashioning Jesus, of reproducing him, but it is one of doing what he did. To act morally and in a Christian manner nowadays, to train in Christian morality nowadays, does not mean handing on with all the veneration and adoration of worship, all the precise details of historical reconstitution and all the precautions of tradition, the embalmed mummy of the moral revolution brought about by Jesus. It means doing in our world what he did in his. But it also means doing in our religious world, in the world of our religion, what he did in his. In regard to morals—what we might call the credibility of the *Christian* faith—does not exist because of the genuine accordance of Christian morals with cultural, socio-economic, political and even religious orders. The credibility of Christian faith in regard to morals, the fact that it is truly Christian, that is to say, that it lives by the Spirit that was the Spirit of Jesus and which Jesus bestowed upon it, it that it conforms (and this conformity is always scandalous) with what Jesus said and did, and that it does in its own world what Jesus did in his.

## MORAL EDUCATION BY DINING WITH WHORES

In fact it was with a pharisee that Jesus dined that evening, and perhaps he had breakfast or lunch with him, anyway. The text (Lk. 7:36 *et seq.*) does not say that the woman was at table. But it does say that: 'when she learned that he was at table in the pharisee's house, brought an alabaster flask of ointment, and standing behind him at his feet, weeping, she began to wet his feet with her tears, and wiped them with the hair of her head, and kissed his feet, and anointed them with the ointment'. The accusation brought against Jesus on several occasions was not that he dined with whores but that he ate with sinners. But in the twentieth century it is difficult to imagine the immorality, both religious and civil, which was then in question if a moral Jew ate with sinners. To say nowadays that Jesus ate with sinners is to weaken what was actually at issue, and therefore I get the necessary vehemence by substituting the more shocking term 'whore'.

The same kind of correction is necessary in regard to several categories of people whom Jesus turned to especially: lepers, the lame, the blind, deaf, dumb, and so on. Our Christian piety turns them into respectable and worthy symbols of more or less spiritual difficulties. But in the time of Jesus these people were outcasts, removed more or less to the civil and religious margins of the community, because their physical affliction was more or less explicitly connected with a moral evil which gave them an aura of suspicion. A person of good morals would keep his distance from them and content himself with almsgiving. *A fortiori* the same was true of those whose profession seemed so depraved that they were often referred to in no greater detail than as 'sinners', hence they appear together with the term sinners as if in a litany both in the gospels and in the Judaic texts of the period: 'publicans and sinners', 'publicans and prostitutes', 'the unjust, adulterers, publicans', 'tax-gatherers, bandits, money-changers, publicans', and so on. After having carefully outlined the religious, civil and moral vetos accorded these different categories, J. Jeremias concludes: 'We can sum up by saying that those about Jesus included first and foremost those who were victims of public contempt . . . uncultured and ignorant people whose *religious* ignorance and *moral* conduct [stressed by Jeremias] denied them, according to contemporary conviction, access to salvation'.[2]

In consorting with all these people in such a way that he was so often reproached for eating with tax-collectors and sinners (Mt. 9:11), of being a glutton and a drunkard, a friend of tax-collectors and sinners (Mt. 11:19), of receiving sinners and eating with them (Lk. 15:2), and retorting to the pharisees: 'Truly, I say to you, the tax-collectors and the harlots go into the kingdom of God before you' (Mt. 21:31), Jesus' primary concern certainly was not morals, because what he was above all concerned with was a revelation about God. It was a question for him of showing who God is, and that he is not such that his manifestation and encounter are subject to the restrictions and vetos which said that, according to the doctors and priests, then as now, that those people had no right to God on the pretext of their *moral* conduct and their *religious* ignorance. But if morality is not primarily in question, it is in question as is moral training.

Similarly, when in the parable of the good Samaritan, Jesus substitutes a Samaritan for the third term of the traditional Jewish trio: a priest, a levite and an Israelite, what is primarily in question is a revelation about God, for it is primarily in regard to God that Jews and Samaritans were divided. Here too it is a question of saying who God is. And the scandal was the same as saying to a Samaritan woman that God was of such a nature that he was not subject to such divisions: ' "Woman, believe me, the hour is coming when neither on this mountain nor in Jerusalem will you worship the Father' (Jn. 4:21, 23). But even if morals are not primarily in question, they *are* in question, as is moral education. Because to say that and to behave in that way are to say what it is necessary to do in order to live the life that has to be lived because it is the life of God himself given in participation to man: the life from which the Living God wishes man to live and which He wants to share with him.

If all this raises the question of morals and of moral training, it is not so because Jesus was indicating that adultery, theft, the oppression of the poor, and ignorance of the Law are good things or matters of indifference as far as God is concerned. On the contrary, on several occasions he expressed himself on these subjects with greater severity than those whom he was criticizing and who criticized him. It is because what has to be done if God is to be God among men and if his Kingdom is to come, is not primarily to reinforce the wall outside which the sinner is cast and which serves to keep him in the same state. Before, and even more than, freeing the sinner from his sin, it is a question of freeing him from the servitude comprised in the judgment that he and his society pronounce on his condition.

Here we come close to what is both the most scandalous and the most specific aspect of the revolution brought about by Jesus in morality. Before reaching that point, it is well to note, as in regard to the sermon on the mount, that to practise morals nowadays and to educate to morality nowadays can only be done in a way that can justly be called Christian and referred to the person who Jesus was, if something is done which represents in our civil, social and religious world nowadays what was represented by Jesus' extraordinary, atypical moral transgression of the civil, social and religious categories which purported to say who had a right to God and who did not because they purported to say who was good and who was bad.

In regard to morals, the credibility of *Christian* faith is not established primarily by its accordance with categories laid down by social, political, economic and even religious orders in order to say who is good and who is not, who has a right to the reward which virtue deserves and who is entitled to the punishment which vice deserves, but by its conformity with the conditions under which Jesus transgressed the categories of this kind which existed in his society in order to be able to say who his God was and his full right to treat with loving-kindness those whom people tried to separate from him.

Here again, it is not a matter of repeating what Jesus did, but of imitating it. The divisions brought about by our societies, and our economic, cultural, moral and religious systems, are not the same as those of Jesus' time. But it is our duty, if we call ourselves Christians, to do in regard to our divisions what he did in relation to his. Otherwise we shall be repeating indefinitely what Jesus in his time said to John the Baptist's messengers about what he was doing: 'the blind receive their sight and the lame walk, lepers are cleansed and the deaf hear, and the dead are raised up, and the poor have good news preached to them' (Mt. 11:5). But we shall have said nothing to those whom our society treats as blind, or whom it makes blind, those whom its treats as lame or whom it makes lame, those whom it treats as poor or whom it makes poor, those whom it treats as dead or whom it makes dead. To be sure we shall not have given offence to anyone, or to any established order—or any established disorder. But why did Jesus close his message to John the Baptist with the words: 'Blessed is he who takes no offence at me!'?

## GOD IS NOT A REWARD FOR VIRTUE

But in regard to what his environment felt to be not moral formation but a deformation of morals, Jesus did worse, or better. He treated sin and the sinner in a way exactly contrary to that required by what is currently known as morals. Every reasonable system, every reasonable form of moral education, would have treated Zacchaeus, the woman taken in adultery, the prostitute who kissed his feet, and so on, in a quite different way. On observing the immorality in which all these people lived, every responsible system of moral education would begin by saying: God is a God of infinite mercy, come to save the one who is lost (up to that point Jesus is on the right road), his greatest desire is that you should come back to him. To that end and in order to be able to meet so great a love, you must begin by banishing the immorality from your life and restoring everything to conformity with the moral order. Then God will be able to encounter you anew. In short, if Jesus had behaved in accordance with the normal laws of customary moral training, he would have said to Zacchaeus: 'Zacchaeus, come down quick, I am coming to your house today (up to that point Jesus was on the right road, cf. Lk. 19:6); but since you have cheated so many people and robbed so many of the poor, start by giving back what you have taken from them. Then I shall be able to come to see you as I wish!'

In the same way Jesus would normally have had to say to the adultress: 'I condemn you, because adultery is worthy of condemnation and personally I condemn it even more severely than the law of Moses. But if you promise me not to sin again, if you lead a life required by the moral law, then I will forgive you'. Similarly, before allowing this sinner to kiss his feet, to anoint them with ointment and to wipe them with her hair, he should have asked her for a reckoning, and a promise that she would put her life to rights.

But, as we know, he did not behave in anything like that way. He did not ask anything from the woman whose presence would have been much less shocking if she had been a repentant sinner, and nothing in the text says that she had ceased her trade or that she had begun by telling Jesus that she intended to do so. Everything, on the contrary, would seem to show that she was still considered as an active sinner. The adultress did not express any desire to amend her life or to repent, any more than Zacchaeus. And Jesus did not ask that of them.

That is inconceivable. And no one wants to believe it. Spontaneously we reintroduce into the 'moral lesson' that we draw from these texts the usual, the normal lesson: the lesson that respects the *status quo*. The sinner has no right to forgiveness; he has no right to God unless he begins by expressing his contrition, unless he is punished first or he punishes himself, or in any case that he does penance. It is the penance performed by the sinner that makes possible forgiveness and a new meeting with God.

But Jesus always behaved in a precisely opposite way. He himself entered into the new encounter, without setting any preliminary condition. He re-established the relationship with the man or woman who had been excluded, not by telling them that they were not sinners or that sin was not important, but by telling them who God is simply by approaching them. Penitence or the call to penitence comes then as a consequence of the re-established encounter; it is a fruit of the re-established encounter, a fruit of what amounted to the entire initiative on Jesus' side. It is *after* and not *before* that Zacchaeus gives a half of his goods to the poor and makes someone give back four times what he has extorted. It is *after* saying to her: 'I do not condemn you', that Jesus says to the adultress: 'Go and sin no more' (Jn. 8:11), instead of saying to her *beforehand:* 'I condemn you, but if you are determined not to sin again, I shall not condemn you any more, so go!' The sequence is not: (*a*) the sinner says that he is a sinner and confesses his sin; (*b*) he does penance; (*c*) consequently, God can once again be God in regard to him. The sequence is the exact opposite: (*a*) Jesus says who God is, and shows how God is God with this woman, and with this man; (*b*) the sinner is restored to God's company; (*c*) the sinner confesses his sin and does penance. It is the manifestation of the way in which God is love which brings about the conversion and not the conversion which allows God to allow his love free play.

That is the contrary, and the exact contrary, of the way in which our morals, our societies and our religions, but also our personal psychological reactions, whether conscious or unconscious, think that guilt ought to be treated. The moral education given by Jesus does not consist in first of all making clear the evil of sin and showing how virtue is to be recommended; it begins by showing who God is, and without any prior condition. The God of Jesus Christ is not a reward that religion would be bound to give to the virtuous and to deny to sinners. If Christianity wishes to be a *Christian* religion, that is, to imitate what Jesus did, it should treat the adultress, the prostitute, the publican, as Jesus treated them, and not as they are automatically treated by various civil, social, moral and even religious systems. The God of Jesus Christ is not a reward for the repentant sinner. It is on the contrary the repentant sinner who seems to be a reward for God, if we are to believe what is said in so many parables.

There has been much debate in recent years on the specific content of Christian morality. There has also been discussion about the specific nature of Christian moral formation: education or training. The fear that what is specific to Christianity will be diluted has been all the greater because certain moral values that were originally specifically Christian are henceforth values practiced by everyone, or in any case acknowledged by everyone, whether Christian or not, whether believers or not. Faced with this dilution, or rather this universalization of Christian moral values, there has been a tendency to react by insisting on what French pastoral theology has in the last few years termed the demands of the Gospel. The nub of their complaint is that in the midst of various non-Christian moralities professing the same values as Christianity, the originality of Christianity should have been more obvious. To use an analogy from athletics, Christianity would like to set the bar higher, and one would have to be, or in any case would want to be, high-jump champion of morality in order to be a Christian. That is not so strange, for of course the sermon on the mount sets the bar very high.

But we have to ask why we have really looked so ineffectively for what is specific to Christian morality, and consequently Christian moral education, in the quite specific attitudes of what Jesus was, and which should therefore be accordingly just as specific to Christianity: dining with whores, and not making God a reward for the just but making what was lost a reward for God.

*Translated by V. Green*

## Notes

1. Quoted by J. Jeremias, *Neutestamentliche Theologie,* vol. I (1971). This work has inspired my present reflections at several points.
   2. *Op. cit.,* p. 144.

# PART III

*The Situation of the Ecclesial Society in Moral*
*Formation*

Johannes Neumann

# Rights and Duties of Ecclesial Society

## THE SITUATION

THE modern period is marked by the collapse of united value and meaning systems which has come to be a sign of enlightened emancipation. In a situation in which everyone can become 'blessed in his fashion' there can be no absolutely valid system of values and meaning that everyone has to acknowledge. Hence the pluralist society is determined by a multitude of competitive (and to some extent fiercely competitive) value and meaning systems. In this process the determination of the contents of values and meanings is either very prominent (leisure, consumption and so forth) or vague (welfare, individual well-being and so forth). To a considerable extent, these partial values are so cleverly manipulated as required by interested powers (industry and/or the mass media) that this is often unknown to the individual. That is how 'one' lives.

Reason nevertheless presupposes the experience of such values as loyalty, patience, kindness and forgiveness. Nowadays this is made difficult if not impossible by the rhythm of work and the hectic nature of leisure pursuits.

External influences have often turned the individual consciousness of good and evil into a vapid hedonism. Responsibility for the other, for one's neighbour or for the community (a town, a people or a nation) has to a great extent given way to indifference or resignation. The collectives in factories, in a sports stadium, in works canteens and apartment blocks are too dense for anything like a form of communal reference with an individual emphasis to arise. The individual disappears in the mass.[1]

On the other hand that very feeling of being on one's own and of powerlessness encourages profound anxieties which can suddenly burst out in expressions of aggressive solidarity. Since moreover the existing political parties and the traditional interest blocks have largely grown corrupt and are therefore lacking in credibility, clever demogogues find a ready audience. This is all the more the case inasmuch as the phenomenon of reduced gratification set expectations and claims in industrial mass societies ever higher and it is just as hard for those in power to confess that the barriers of growth and feasibility have to a great extent already been reached as for the 'consumers' to accept the same truth. Constantly increasing expectations and requirements make too great demands on our social and industrial systems. On the other hand, our economic and financial cycle depends to a large extent on ever-new stimuli to consumption and from the arousal of ever-new expectations and longings whose fulfilment is promised.

Nevertheless it is not excluded that one day every man and woman has to face pain and suffering or death, whatever trouble is taken by our present-day society to remove these phenomena consistently from conscious perception. Hence these 'blows of fate' find men fully unprepared when they strike him. He is unadjusted to them and has not in any way taken into account their application to him personally. The question of the meaning of one's own existence now suddenly comes up and frequently reveals the depths of inner emptiness. Non-sense appears to be the meaning of all existence when all hedonistic and superficial maxims no longer seem to offer any solace.

On the other hand we experience how, after some deep-reaching national calamity, something affects a nation that one can, quite credibly, call a 'folk conscience'. A process of that kind would seem to be taking place at present in the United States. After the moral and military catastrophe of Vietnam and the political cynicism of Watergate, the American people elected a President with a moralizing bent. He tries to apply ethical principles in politics, the economy and social life. It remains to be seen whether and how far he will succeed in producing in this regard a consensus regarding moral values in public life and through the public. This current phenomenon in the United States has its many analogies in the human rights movements in the socialist countries and the civil rights movements in western countries. Nowadays people seem to be more open to such ethically motivated actions than in Kennedy's time, since his call to make for new shores certainly impressed with its moral sensibility but did not 'come off' among people in any real way.[2]

On the other hand, it should have been clear since the Nazi takeover in Germany in 1933 that neither the dedication of the 'moral forces' of a nation and its emergence from collapse and shame, nor talk of its national rebirth are good in themselves and necessarily lead to good things. If such movements of 'national awakening' do not ensure the dignity of *all* citizens and people and other freedoms to be different and to think differently, the danger inheres in these 'popular movements' that they will not make people better but impel them to mass agression.

Contemporary examples should show that there are sometimes widely distributed impulses to a new ethical awakening. One has to ask however whether and how far these concerns go beyond mere stimuli, and whether they are then directed by values: in other words, whether they seek to improve the actual condition of mankind, and help him to live a truly happy life in freedom among free men.

## WHAT CAN THE CHURCH DO IN VIEW OF THIS SITUATION?

To be sure the Church cannot and should not exclusively and primarily understand its task as consolation and help for human needs. Otherwise it would misapply itself as 'opiate for the people'. Instead it has to bear witness to the good news of the Word of God made man in his saving and consoling as well as his encouraging and stirring fulness. It is certainly there above all for the weary and heavy laden, for the sinners and unjust, yet its task is essentially more inclusive and broader: to enable man to become a new creation in Christ in the power of the Spirit, not through its arts and achievements but through the *promise* given to it. Hence it is in an ambivalent position. Its task is to announce the word of the Lord. Its concern is for men and what we are accustomed to call their 'salvation'. On the one hand it can by its nature only achieve those two things as a community, as a people called by God, just as on the other hand it can never look on man only as an individual but must always take into consideration his complex involvement in society. Therefore it is also *fundamentally* charged with responsibility for actual human society as well as for the individual.

The Church today lives in large areas of the world in states which, at least according to the phrasing of their constitutions, wish to be neutral as far as religion and world view are concerned. One of their main tasks should be to guarantee the freedom of religious and political conviction, especially the freedom of conscience of the individual as well as of social bodies. The actual external forms and areas of freedom thus guaranteed are of course very different in practice.

It is fundamentally important that the decision for this basic attitude on the part of states already includes a specific 'decision of conscience' and an option for specific values: namely the recognition of the freedom of religious and political conviction and of conscience of the citizen with their varying notions. That implies the making of very specific value decisions. But how are they to be justified?

That is certainly not to be effected in a purely legal and positivistic way with the statement that in most states these rights are—formally at least—guaranteed by positive (constitutional) law. Instead we should start from the fact that in these value notions established according to legal norms, a position is expressed which represents the result of a long spiritual, intellectual and political history of development, working to form consciences and determine values. At the same time we have to admit that in this regard the Church often is and was not very helpful in practice, because on the basis of its ontological thinking it is (and was) wont to distinguish *absolutely* between truth and error. In this regard it claimed to be the *only source* of definition of what actually counted as truth and error. This attitude prevented it from acknowledging a legitimate majority of political and religious convictions and from defending spiritual and political tolerance. Only external circumstances forced the Church to take notice of the presence of other political and religious entities and finally to recognize them, at the second Vatican Council, as a positive and meaningful development.[3]

The essential impulse to this new viewpoint was not only political opportunism, but a new valuation of the dignity of the human person as a being that can and must be responsible for him or herself.[4]

The long delayed dialogue between the Catholic Church and the world which Pope Leo XIII had already interested himself in (even if partly on the basis of inadequate and inappropriate presuppositions) and which Pope Pius XII had tried to take further, Pope John XXIII not only energetically promoted, but gave a direction to. If the encyclical *Mater et Magistra* of 15 May 1961[5] set its sights above all on social questions, the encyclical *Pacem in terris* of 11 April 1963[6] took *all* areas of human life as its theme. All human communal life is only to be seen as well ordered, fruitful and in accordance with human dignity, if it is grounded on truth and is developed in unlimited freedom to the point of a harmony which is worthy of human beings (nn. 28 ff).

Pope Paul VI also tried in his first encyclical, *Ecclesiam Suam* of 10 August 1964,[7] to answer the question *how* the dialogue between the Church and men of our time was to be conducted. The Council took up these papal stimuli and tried to put them into words. In so doing it intended its pronouncements as keynotes and not as a finished work. The pastoral constitution *Gaudium et spes* on the Church in the modern world is intended to be critical assessment and responsible self-reflection within and invitation to dialogue and cooperation without.

The Church in no way claims to make absolute pronouncements. Instead it tries to show the signs of the times in the light of the Gospel, in order to give the present generation an answer in an appropriate way (art. 4). Technology, science and politics are recognized as independent areas of human development, but also of great personal responsibility. The present-day problems of personalization and socialization are considered and responsibly reflected on. This constitution's analysis of the situation in terms of psychological, moral and religious changes, is realistic and to the point in a way hardly experienced to date in any ecclesiastical document. The Council takes note of the current trend 'in which doubt seems to have become public opinion'[8] but without itself getting stuck in a description of this doubt situation. It sees clearly that in many countries not only the theories of the philosophers but also to a great extent literature, art, the interpretations of science and history and even of civil law are permeated with an atheism that has already become obvious (art. 7).

The pastoral constitution *Gaudium et spes* presents a programme for the help which the Church has to offer the individual as well as human society, and how it is to support human concern for a more humane world (art. 41–3). In these different ways it is trying through its various branches and as a whole to make an essential contribution to forming the possibilities of human life (art. 40).

The great significance and predictive value of this constitution is almost certainly that in it the Church for the first time in an official text consistently recognizes the 'rights of man' and the 'thrust of the present age which advances those rights everywhere' (art. 41).

Today the Church wishes to contribute to the assurance and development of human rights. For the dignity of the human person made in the image of God offers standards for an inclusive 'liberation' of man, a 'liberation' that must not be mistaken for either a 'false autonomy' or a cynical libertinism. Unfortunately the constitution offers no substantial explanation of what we are to understand under 'dignity of the human person' or where the 'false autonomy' of men begins. Only that attitude is decisively rejected which starts from the assumption that the personal rights of man are only fully guaranteed 'if we are absolutely free of all norms of divine law'.

Hence the Church sees it as its task to recall in human attempts to interpret value and meaning, the facts of the human dignity and 'liberated freedom' with which God has endowed man, and to measure the thrust of human self-liberation by those yardsticks. For that purpose the Church needs a measure that is not only ontologically calibrated but takes into account historical change, rational emancipation and socio-economic progress. In other words: the Church must become aware that nowadays, after Galileo, Kant, Hegel, Marx, Hiroshima, and in view of the danger of atomic warfare and industrial and economic suasions, as well as the threat of a planned and bureaucratized world, interpretations of the world have to differ from those of previous epochs. Both the Church as a whole and individual believers should beware the danger of seeing in a naively optimistic manner the manipulable aspects of atomic energy or the 'planning rationality' of 'perfect' bureaucratic computer control an (ultimate) fulfilment of its task of making the earth subject to it (Gen. 1:28). That kind of assessment of human capabilities is something that in fact the Church should be exposing as a dangerous utopia in the spirit of the Tower of Babel. It should not support or advance this *hubris* in any way. Instead the Church must stimulate mankind's self-critical conscience.

## THE POSITION OF THE CHURCH'S PARTNERS

Even when we do not think that tactical and diplomatic action is appropriate to the Church, the (Catholic) Church nevertheless has to pursue its actual course according to diverse social situations. These circumstances may be determined by a particular legal set-up or con-situation and/or by specific emotional premises. The following are basic situations in which the Church has to bear witness to the good news entrusted to it:[9]

1. The Church lives as *religio illicita* in states in which 'religious freedom' is aggressively interpreted as 'freedom from religion'. Here the good news can often take effect only when hidden in men's hearts. In these cases it has to deal with increasingly refined and inhuman techniques of repression which know how to remove even the sign of martyrdom from public life.[10]

2. The Church comes under suspicion as a (former) colonial overlord or as the expression of European colonialism and finds its freedom of action considerably reduced. Here only the thorny way is possible of showing that the Church is concerned with man and his salvation and not with power and domination.

3. In accordance with another cultural and religious tradition, a (so-called pagan) religion holds sway as the state religion. Then the Christian Church can take part only in activities relating to foreigners or ethnic minorities. In this situation the quiet presence and selfless witness of Christian love are the only possibility of proclamation.

4. Because the Church—or a major part of it—because of certain social conditions, has to stand up for the poor and repressed, either as a

whole or in certain instances—without any notice being taken of any existing constitutional or legal guarantees—it is persecuted and repressed. Then the support of the oppressed can be fatal. But that does not mean that it is not to be recommended; without such a course the Christian Gospel would be lacking in credibility in such situations.

5. On the basis of the state constitution there is a *total* separation between the state and every religious organization. In this legal situation church activity is for the most part not (essentially) restricted, yet the Church receives no public support. Under these conditions the Church can take its own dynamic course more or less independently and participate like any other (private) society in legal life, the formation of political conscience and social life, insofar as its activity is legitimated by the support of its faithful.

6. Although the state and Church are fundamentally separate and there is no state Church, the Church nevertheless enjoys in law as well as in practice a more or less considerable special position and at the same time complete freedom of internal affairs. Under a legal system of this kind which allows the Church a certain special legal and social position, according it something of the status of a corporate entity in public law, and official assistance from state organs, for instance in the collecting of church tax, the Church is free from state interference or any obstacle. Nevertheless a certain amplitude of means and an obvious socio-political influence can lead the Church to a false assessment of its real position.

7. The Church possesses (*de jure* or *de facto*) more or less the advantages of a 'state religion'. The price paid for such a more or less inclusive state 'patronage' consists in dependence on governmental will and in an identification with the existing political system that is dangerous for the Church. The result can be that the Catholic people (the basis) have spiritual and material concerns that the hierarchy and priests (want or ought to) know nothing about. Such a system, that considerably reduces the Church's freedom, ultimately damages proclamation more in the long run than total separation would.

It may be superfluous to state that in each of the above groups there are various differences in emphasis from country to country.

Hence it is impossible to lay down universally valid rules for church behaviour, spiritual proclamation and social presence. Of course the task of bearing witness, of proclaiming the good news, remains the same everywhere and always, yet the manner and kind of ways in which they are realized can be fundamentally different.

Unfortunately, under political conditions as indicated under heads 4 to 7 above, the Church on the spot, represented by episcopate, clergy and faithful, can try to make its rights prevail and to make the fruits of the good news of Jesus take effect in a particular society.

In answering the question of the Church's position, a fundamental distinction has to be made between its legally ordained relation to the state as such and its effectiveness in society. It is conceivable that in spite of a legally preferential position in regard to the state, the Church has hardly any influence on social development, just as on the other hand in the case of constitutional separation from the state it nevertheless, or precisely for that reason, can actually exert influence on social life and its development. That means: if political conditions (at least basically) take into account human rights and especially the basic right to religious freedom, the possibility of the Church influencing the processes of public conscience formation and the formation of values is decided less by its legal status than by its spiritual thrust: the credibility of its commitment as grounded in the Gospel and the tenability of its message.

Because both individual states and diverse social systems are necessarily determined by ethical and legal norms, the Church is confronted by partners with differing notions of values and law. It can take up three very different basic positions.

That of a mediator which hands on universally accepted human values; that of a guardian who for the sake of man's divine image not only promotes certain fundamental values but as far as possible decisively represents them; and finally that of a contemporary under challenge who together with others reflects on certain newly arising problems and looks for humanly just solutions to them.

## CHURCH AND STATE

As a major international organization, the Roman Catholic Church enjoys diplomatic relations with some ninety states.[11] On this—culturally and spiritually—far from unproblematic level, the Church is present in the politico-diplomatic area of the state, though not necessarily in social life and in the public consciousness. Here there is hardly any decisive influence on ethically significant solutions to problems or their appropriate treatment. Diplomatic cunning and polite etiquette rule, and political caution is called for. Certain exceptions usually owe their spiritual efficacy to a particular church representative. In most cases, however, church influence on social and ethical questions in this area is almost entirely restricted by considerations which it may seem necessary to take into account and by the relatively small power that can be exercised.

Wherever the Church thinks, however, that favourable circumstances give it a stronger position, until now at least it has hardly used this for the sake of mankind and its freedom, the alleviation of human need and the abolition of human anxieties, but to the advantage of the Church as an institution. The only examples I need cite are the demands for ecclesiastical authority over marriage, Catholic education, chaplaincies in the armed forces, assurance of church possessions, the special position of clergy (freedom from the law, taxation and military service), financial privileges and the like. Not infrequently, when making these demands, the Church wants something morally questionable, for instance when it forbids the state partner in a concordat to retain the possibility of divorce as its own concern, or when it requires state sanctions against certain persons—for instance 'lapsed priests' or 'heretics', or has itself recognized as the state religion (the concordat with Italy in 1929 that with Spain in 1953 may be cited here by way of example). From the viewpoint of evangelical example and aid to conscience formation the *spiritual* value of Vatican diplomacy can certainly not be set very high, even though the Church as a universal institution would not find it easy to dispense with this kind of political communication, and there is undoubtedly a spiritually intended awareness of mission behind all such diplomatic activities.

The influence of a national Catholic Church on public moral consciousness and the political behaviour of its citizens, especially in critical situations, is dependent on too many factors for anything universally valid to be said about it. In general, however, it is true that the official political influence of the church hierarchy frequently prevents the state from enacting legislation that is just, appropriate and cognizant of the interests of *all* citizens. In this regard we have only to recall, for example, the ecclesiastical protests against the enactment of equality before the law in the Federal Republic of Germany, against the introduction of divorce in Italy, and against the necessary reform of education, and penal, marriage and family law in Federal Germany. In these cases the official representatives of the Church always portrayed their traditional interests as universally binding demands of natural or divine law. That not infrequently meant that the state legislature, as a result of what seemed necessary consideration of church reactions, enacted laws that were deficient in form and content. Ten years or so later, however, the decrees brought in by the state in spite of ecclesiastical resistance were often accepted by Catholics too as right and reasonable. In such cases the Church does not form consciences but rather settles them. In fact it prevents the taking of humane and responsible decisions.

In confessedly atheistic systems, which often severely affect the possibility of the Church having any influence or effect, it is hardly possible to avoid cautious contacts with the regime in order to prevent a greater evil. Yet precisely such contacts—whatever level they take place on—not infrequently disappoint the hopes of those who expect from church leaders authentic witness to Christian freedom and an acknowledgment of true—because divinely founded—humanity.[12]

Altogether we may say that politico-diplomatic contacts between the Church and whatever state it is in contribute very little to public or individual conscience formation. Those states which limit the freedom and human rights of their citizens on certain ideological grounds discredit the Church and its work when there are official or even friendly contacts with the hierarchy. If on those occasions a specific moral action is elicited from the state possibly even at the Church's behest, people's inner acceptance of that moral action is made still more questionable.

## CHURCH IN SOCIETY

Real testimony to the Gospel seems possible and effective nowadays only where the Church, as the community of the faithful and not only as the hierarchy, collaborates in basic solidarity in the formation of will and awareness of responsibility in society. The prerequisite for that is that Christians recognize their fellow men's needs and cares as their own and act together with them to resolve problems in a humane, appropriate and realistic manner. The basic and premise of their activity is necessarily belief in the God who has revealed himself historically in Jesus Christ. That demands conviction and loyalty and solidarity with the needs and anxieties of mankind, and sensitivity to the dignity and individual responsibility even of those who think differently as well as of the poor and rejected.

As a rule resolutions and threats have no power to change society. Only credible concern, unreserved commitment and remedial action together with personal application and argumentative advice on the basis of authentic faith can prove convincing. Only on the presupposition of a just common human solidarity based in faith can the Church, acting through its members, help individuals and social institutions responsibly to inform their consciences. Only by acting in concert can modern Christians and non-Christians solve present-day needs, both in employers' organizations and in trade unions and in other social conjunctures. On such occasions Christian have a contribution to make in the form of the hope grounded in Jesus' resurrection. But they have to recognize the fact that the Christian faith is not a simple key to the solution of all social, economic and political problems. They have to become aware that they must contribute to their common concerns and actions unwavering faith in God's promise and hope in his loyalty. Yet that will not reduce the number of problems to be faced. On the contrary, some questions, for instance in regard to the meaning of death and suffering, poverty and cruelty, stand out even more radically and mercilessly.

In the removal of conflicts born of hunger and poverty, illiteracy, spiritual and economic underdevelopment, injustice and traditional enmity, Christians nowadays can no longer restrict themselves to the purely 'religious' proclamation of the Gospel. Instead they have to share their concern with all those who are similarly affected: their concern for the increase of knowledge, of moral responsibility and an improvement of conditions. Their passionate motivation is, however, sustained not by a universal humanity but by faith in the godlike dignity of every single individual. That includes knowledge of the fallibility and unpredictability of human nature. Only in faith can the anxieties be conquered which proceed from the deep contrarieties of life. A Christian will always mistrust the confident optimism of planners and bureaucrats just as much as all promises of total, imminent salvation, whether of political or scientific provenance.

On the basis of the incarnate historicity of the Christian message, Christians can never remain satisfied with the *status quo*. They know in faith that all human conditions are not only subject to development, but also cry out for change, because they are provisional. They believe too that One died for many so that others might have life in new dignity and conscious responsibility. In all their just undertakings they will therefore never be able to forget that even their lords and masters have human faces and therefore share in the godlike dignity of all men. Therefore they will have weighty thoughts upon the subject of whether and on what grounds it is permissible to use force.

In less extreme situations, such as obtain for instance in Australia, in Canada, in some countries of Central Europe, in the USA and other countries that respect rights and laws, Christians are aware that what is 'distinctively Christian' can only take effect socially to the extent that they themselves can be noticed by society and actively engage in it out of faith.

In present-day pluriform societies which seem largely to have lost all sense of non-material values, Christians will be able to contribute to conscience-formation (whether of socially relevant institutions or of individuals) if they are able to distinguish what is generally acceptable, which has to be rationally demonstrable and obvious, from what is the unique content of their faith that enables them to make decisions and distinctions. Above all they have the following to contribute: our contemporary (democratic) systems need acknowledgment and concern for the realization of certain necessary values such as justice, loyalty, peace and trust. Only if a society is capable of weaving such values into a protective though not restrictive covering can the individual citizen find a certain degree of security and the common good prevail. That presupposes that most citizens actually acknowledge such values out of free insight and acceptance. That in its turn demands a considerable degree of political as well as human sagacity and a refusal to pursue one's own interests to the disadvantage of others. An ethically grounded attitude of this kind will only be really vital and voluntary if it is nourished from an ideological yet religious source, however diffuse that might be in the individual. All these human hopes must of course take into account the phenomenon of loss of gratification[13] which usually prevents ultimate satisfaction and allows constantly new wishes to arise after the fulfilment of this one or that one.

Today the great social task of the Church in terms of the common human good, and as far as individuals are concerned, is to a great extent to contribute to the formation and preservation of the necessary concepts of value as well as to the subsequent process of the discovery and elucidation of meaning. In this regard the Church is faced with a difficult task:

On the one hand, in all demonstrations of human solidarity it has to bear witness to Jesus as Lord.

On the other hand, it must not posit as absolute the value-judgments that follow from a religious confession of faith. It must not only ground them in the basis of the godlike dignity of the incarnate Jesus Christ, but it must also ground them, if it is to make their general value accessible, in a general human, historically relevant and socially acceptable form. For even fundamental values are always enclosed in a context of a specific horizon of understanding which demands justice, social security and the same access to justice for all men, and also the recognition of the social indebtedness of property; it must also accord freedom even to those who think or live differently. These premises do not emerge directly from revelation. Instead they are, like the elucidation of what loyalty, morality and peace actually mean, dependent on specific spiritual, intellectual, social and political presuppositions. To a large extent these do not underlie the formative *power* of the Church; rather it has to introduce *the* yardstick: namely the incarnate Jesus Christ as the help and support of the needy, suffering, sick and oppressed, but also of the happy and thankful, and all of those who have a human countenance.

*Translated by V. Green*

## Notes

1. E. Canetti, *Masse und Macht*, two vols. (1960).
2. Cf. J. F. Kennedy's speeches.
3. E. W. Böckenförde describes 'the question of tolerance and freedom of religion' as the 'great way of the cross of western Christianity' (in *Kirchlicher Auftrag und politische Entscheidung* (1973), p. 173. The history of this way can be found in J. Leclerc's article in *Concilium* 2 (1969).
4. Cf. P. Pavan, in *Concilium* 2 (1969) and in *LThK. II. Vat. Konzil. II* (1967), pp. 704 ff.
5. AAS 53 (1961), pp. 401–64.
6. AAS 55 (1963), pp. 257–304.
7. AAS 56 (1964), pp. 609–59.
8. J. Green, cited in *LThK. II. Vat. Konzil III* (1968), p. 303; for the whole question in detail, cf. J. Neuman, 'Das Zusammenwirken von Staat und Kirche' in *Materialdienst der Diözese Rottenburg 3* (1974), pp. 13–27.
9. An up-to-date comprehensive analytical description of the religious-political situation in different parts of the world is lacking. J. Funk in *Die Religion in den Verfassungen der Erde* (1960) tried to provide an overview in 1960. In the meanwhile the actual situation in many parts of the world has changed. Many states have only come into existence since then. For Europe P. Leisching, *Kirche und Staat in den Rechtsordnungen Europas* (1973), provides an informative overview.
10. Compare T. Beeson, *Was drüben möglisch ist. Existenzbedingungen der Kirchen in Osteuropa* (1977).

Miguel Benzo

# Moral Training in Spain from 1939 to 1975

THE aim of this short study is to sum up the predominant moral training in Spain from 1939 to 1975. It is as well to point out at the outset
that any historical situation depends on antecedents which explain it to
a greater or lesser extent; and no historical situation stays the same
during thirty-six years. To take their main outlines, the antecedents of
this period in the aspect that concerns us here can be summed up like
this: since the late Middle Ages the Church in Spain has had an enor-
mous and continuing social influence and as an institution has remained
closely tied to the ruling classes, although part of the rural clergy and
some religious orders have provided admirable examples of identification with the poor. This type of influence was not diminished by the
liberal revolution which in Spain was only effective for short and
sporadic periods.

It was from this position that the Spanish Church had to face up to
the industrial revolution, which came later to Spain than to the major
part of Europe, at the end of the nineteenth century. The Church's
most general reaction was one of incomprehension: its pastoral activity
remained exclusively dedicated to the world of the peasants and the
middle and upper classes, ignoring the growth of an urban proletariat.
The beginning of this century saw a first attempt at 'social Catholicism'
inspired by the papal teachings of the time and led mainly by the
Catholic Association of Propagandists, founded in 1908, whose first
president was the then lawyer and secular journalist, later to become
priest, bishop and cardinal, Angel Herrera. His views and that of the
movement seem very conservative today. A new attempt at evangeliz-

ing the working classes 'from within' did not appear until 1945 with the foundation of movements of workers' Catholic Action, which were cut off in their prime in 1966 by the Spanish hierarchy who feared the consequences of their early clashes with the Franco government of the time. Somewhat later some parishes began limited experiments specifically designed to cater for the needs of working-class areas and of worker priests.

This age-long link between the Church and the ruling classes has produced a deep feeling of anti-clerical resentment in the Spanish people. This first appeared centuries ago in stories, proverbs and popular songs and was quite compatible with a deep Catholic faith. It was only at the end of the last century that the liberal parties and the workers made systematic use of this anti-clericalism as a political force, giving it a clearly anti-religious slant.

The coming of the Second Republic in 1931 was generally received with the deepest repugnance among the upper reaches of the clergy and with a certain amount of sympathy among a large part of the lower clergy. But the Republicans made the grave political mistake of not building on this sympathy. Instead they attacked all religious manifestations indiscriminately: the massive burning of churches and convents a month after the proclamation of the Republic, the forbidding of religious to undertake any sort of teaching, the suppression of clerical stipends, the dissolution of the Jesuits, the expulsion of the conservative primate Cardinal Segura, the establishment of divorce, and so on: all produced a wide religious reaction which was rapidly capitalized by the political parties of the Right. At the same time as this confrontation with the lively religious feeling of many Spaniards, the Republicans tried to limit the privileges of the landowners and other major capitalists and some of those of the armed forces, for which they lacked any real strength. Together with the regime's inability to maintain public order, this produced civil war. The Francoist uprising was well received by most of the bishops and the Catholic clergy and people, with the main exception of the Basque nationalists.

AN ETHIC OF ORDER

## Authoritarianism

The experience of the Civil War was a terrible trauma for all those who lived through it, whether on the Republican or the Nationalist side, and gave rise to a general desire for security. This is the only basis on which the subsequent identification of secular society with the Church and the type of moral education that stemmed from it can be understood. The Spain that emerged from the Civil War was anxious for order and stability at any price. This means that it wanted authority—political authority and theological authority. During the war itself Nationalist propaganda had spread a very simple ideology through all the means of communication: a manicheism in which the good principle had several faces and names: religion, order, unity, authority, tradition, Empire (the incredible slogan 'through the Empire to God' was even officially supported) . . . and the bad principle was called Marxism, masonry, atheism, subversion, political parties, separatism. This was what years later came to be called National-Catholicism. This was to be a simple key with which one could interpret everything divine and everything human: the whole of history was nothing other than the endless struggle between these two supreme principles. In the face of the threat of chaos represented by the second principle, which was trying to destroy the recently restored order, the only defence was a monolithic authority on every level: State, Church, family, culture, university, communication, media . . . . So the key to the moral training that was supposedly given during this period of Spanish history can be summed up like this: anything that strengthens obedience to the constituted authority is good; anything that lessens this obedience is bad. This was of course the official theory: its effects were not always by any means what its promoters claimed. Also, acceptance of such authoritarianism lessened as the memory of the Civil War receded into the distance.

## The Social Ethic

The consequences of this authoritarianism in the sphere of public morality can easily be foreseen:

—Obedience to and respect for authorities and official modes of thought (including profession of the Catholic faith) were inculcated as virtues and any sign of discrepancy, criticism or originality was looked on with suspicion.

—The 'structural sins' which favoured the ruling classes were ignored, hidden and excused. Amongst these were the existence of a clearly regressive system of taxation which bore most heavily on the less well-off (which in turn produced a general climate of tax evasion since everyone was convinced of the injustice of the system). Economic corruption at the highest level was ignored: the great financial scandals were punished less heavily than petty theft. In order to obtain any post one needed the recommendation of someone in a position of power, even though this was manifestly unjust.

—The social class exposed to the greatest degree of control and vigilance was of course the working class, considered most capable of producing the greatest threat of subversion: genuinely representative trade unions and strikes were forbidden.

—As for the communications media, censorship suppressed any unfavourable judgment on the behaviour of civil, ecclesiastical and military authorities.

## Family Ethics

The dominant family ideal in the period under review was characterized first and foremost by the claim to undisputed paternal authority. Its outward sign was physical cohesion: the wife and children under age were supposed to be away from the home as little as possible. Civil divorce was suppressed, and laws passed that reinforced paternal authority to the greatest degree possible.

In particular, women (wives and daughters) were supposed to be kept in a situation of dependence. Legislation clearly discriminated against women's economic independence and professional work. The growing and unstoppable tendency, despite contrary pressures, for women to take a job outside the home was looked on with suspicion. Husbands, however, could humourously allow their wives to manage them, but only in an indirect and outwardly affectionate way, never disagreeing openly with them. Large families were rewarded with national prizes and considerable reductions in school fees and fares on public transport. A sociological study showed the exceptionally high average number of children born to ministers in the Franco governments. The sale of contraceptives was rigorously controlled, which produced a black market in them. Legislation against abortion was very severe, despite which it was calculated that there were some 300,000 voluntary abortions every year.

## Sexual Ethics

This period of Spanish history was characterized by an excessive official puritanism which, as always, did not reflect a real puritanism. Sexuality was repressed above all in that it represented an individual rebellion against social authority and cohesion and against paternal authority in the home. As far as the first aspect is concerned, ridiculous extremes were reached: all shows were subject to very strict 'censorship boards' on which ecclesiastics always sat; the rules governing dress on beaches and in swimming baths were very strict but despite this some confessional organizations still saw fit to organize private beaches and swimming baths in which mixed bathing was forbidden; photographs in newspapers and reviews were carefully screened; the only books with sexual information allowed were few and far between and out-of-date.

This repression of sexuality as a sign of autonomy reached its highest peak in the bosom of the family. In the immense majority of families it was implicitly supposed that the only active protagonist of sexuality was the father. The wife was allotted a passive role to the extent that many husbands considered that acceptance of sexual relations demanded a 'sacrifice' on the part of their wives, a sacrifice which had to be rewarded with gifts and special considerations (an idea which some wives exploited more or less consciously). Fathers refused to accept that their children could have their own sexual problems: so any sort of sexual education was excluded. The law forbade co-education in primary and secondary schools. This and the ruling social customs made the first contacts between the sexes difficult and precarious. Society rejected any sort of physical intimacy between engaged couples. For an unmarried daughter to become pregnant was considered one of the greatest possible social disgraces.

Alongside this family puritanism society allowed and even exalted 'machismo': that is, the belief that certain qualities (physical courage, daring, energy, insolence) and the dominion of the man over the woman are natural consequences of being a man. One manifestation of this mentality is 'Donjuanismo': not only was this socially accepted but a certain admiration was even accorded to the man who had sexual adventures—always provided that he did not invade the marital and paternal territory of another man: hence the tolerance of a more or less institutionalized prostitution.

### SIGNS OF EVOLUTION

## From the Ethic of Poverty to the Ethic of Development

During the period under review Spain has progressed from being an underdeveloped industrial nation to one that is well on the way of development. This, as in other countries, has produced a change in the generally accepted scale of values. To take one example: for centuries (especially in the more backward regions such as Andalusia and Extremadura) hospitality to a stranger was a widespread and primordial virtue. The massive influx of tourists changed hospitality into a business. To put foreigners up freely in one's own home became ridiculous when everyone else was becoming rich in the hotel trade. The result has been the disappearance of hospitality from the scale of values. Another example: in a poor country in which well-paid work is hard to find, austerity, stoicism in the face of need and the aesthetic use of leisure are highly valued qualities. There is a favourable climate for the production of popular arts with little economic value, such as song and dance (one thinks of *flamenco*), pottery, weaving, and so on. In a wealthy country, on the other hand, leisure disappears and popular art is commercialized, adapting itself to the souvenir trade—much less refined in its products than those that spring from a long professional tradition. These are only two of many possible examples of this sort of change.

In general and with a certain amount of exaggeration, one might say that the ethical ideal of Spaniards has gone from that of the haughty, austere, aloof, courageous, cunning, creative, hospitable, independent individual to that of the hard-working, effective, responsible, prudent, saving citizen, a lover of comfort and a conformist.

## Religiosity

The absolute political regimes that called themselves Catholic by definition produce three types of religiosity: of identification, of evasion and of dissent. The religiosity of identification accepts the regime's confessional claim and requires its believers to collaborate fully with it and so steadily reinforce its position. Inspired by this spirit (and in many cases obviously by their own ambitions), Christians, including ecclesiastics, accept important political offices and thereby support the regime in question, committing themselves to it, which makes an attitude of critical distancing ever more difficult. As the presence of Christians in the government produces in practice some good and in particular avoids some evils, those who have chosen this way feel justified in doing so. In exchange for the support on the part of Catholics, the regime makes considerable concessions to the Church, which in their turn serve to bind the Church ever more closely to it. In the years following the Civil War a system of identification between State and Church was set up: the Council of the Realm, the Cortez, the Council of State, the syndicates, all the organizations of the National Movement (the Youth Front, the feminine section, social assistance, etc.), radio and television, religious offices attached to various ministries and so on. The State paid the clergy salaries, subsidised seminaries and clerical universities, paid for the repair of churches. Teaching of the Catholic religion was obligatory at every level from primary school to university (it has just been stopped in the latter, although in fact it had lapsed some time earlier). The bishops, backed up by the secular arm, exercised a very real and effective authority over clergy and faithful.

The stage of predominance of the religiosity of identification was followed in Spain by that of predominance of the religiosity of evasion. Faced with the impossibility of approving everything done by the regime and the growing tensions created by the steadily increasing opposition, many Christians opted for a purely spiritualist religiosity, that is one centred on the strictly sacral, with a purely individual ethical standpoint lacking any reference to the problems of society. This division of conscience allowed them to consider themselves fervent Christians, while at the same time benefitting from the privileges the political situation gave to their social class. Charismatic movements arose, seeing Pentecostal enthusiasm as a way to forget the menace of social changes and as a way to sublimate their own bad consciences. Groups structured like sects also made their appearance, professing blind obedience to the traditions of the founder, to the superior and to the spiritual director together with a soothing ritualism.

The religiosity of dissent began to gain importance in the nineteen fifties. Those who professed it believed that the model of social ethics derived from Christian principles did not coincide with the type of society put forward by the ruling political regime. They therefore saw more or less active opposition as a duty and considered themselves bound to constant criticism, pointing out the failings in what had been achieved; they became the voice of those who had no voice and the practical defenders of human rights. This attitude was strongly opposed by the public authorities who regarded these Christians as 'traitors', and at its outset was equally opposed by the hierarchy of the Church. Later, however, the Holy See began to appoint bishops whose attitude was at least moderately in favour of this tendency, thereby giving rise to tensions between the regime and the Church. In some cases these non-conformist believers sought to identify their particular dissenting political views with the only views consistent with Christian principles, thereby falling into a new type of identification.

### CONCLUSIONS

Throughout its history, the Catholic Church as a human institution (and presumably other Churches and other religions) has time and again fallen back into the same error, whose pastoral consequences have generally been disastrous: this is the error of allowing its more or less explicit adherence to a political regime or political party to be bought in exchange for certain safeguards, aid and facilities for its work of evangelization. The mechanics of events have always been the same: after a period of persecution, or at least of difficulties placed in its way by a particular group in power, the Church, tired and drugged, has seen that another political group, opposed to the first, offered it the prospect of peace and material help for the exercise of its apostolate in exchange for its support in taking power. Time and again, with a consistency worthy of a better cause, the hierarchy, clergy and the Catholic faithful in general have been caught in the trap: they have accepted the offer with a sigh of relief; after the victory of their patrons they have set themselves to the task of repairing their damaged trenches; they have built Churches and seminaries, increased the number of clerics and religious . . . and closed their eyes to the defects and injustices of the new rulers. But as these demand unconditional approval of all their decisions as a condition the situation has finally become intolerable: then the Church has tried, timidly at first, and then more energetically, when the first attempt is rejected, to criticize the evils of the situation and set itself free from a tutelage that has become oppressive. This in turn produces indignation on the part of the Church's protectors-controllers, who feel they have been cheated and betrayed. Then a new saviour appears: another political grouping intent on taking over from the ruling system promises the Church a greater recognition of its autonomy and greater support in its tasks, and so the vicious circle starts all over again.

After three centuries of persecution, Constantine offered peace to the Christians who had become so numerous and influential in the Empire, and the Church, with some honourable exceptions, closed its eyes to the atrocities committed by the Emperor and his successors. Something similar happened with the Barbarian invasions: after seeing the danger of being swept away by the pagan Aryan torrent, the Church accepted the successive conversions of different rulers with joy and did not look too closely at their crimes, rapine and extortions.

During the Middle Ages the situation was different: the Church was no longer a support to the powers of this world, but had itself become the greatest of the feudal powers. This situation led to the break-up of Christendom with the great Schism of the East and the Protestant Reformation. Catholics and Reformers identified with their respective sovereigns to fight against each other in the atrocious religious wars which devastated Europe, and to set up the dreaded tribunals against deviations from orthodoxy, which served at the same time as a defence of the State and as a badly-understood defence of the Church.

Faced with the Enlightenment and revolution, the Church in the eighteenth and nineteenth centuries generally sided with absolute monarchies and the most conservative politicians with the result that the proletariat, a new protagonist on the social scene, was born and grew up as an adversary.

The moral of this simplified story seems to be that the Christian community should accept that it, like its founder, does not exist to be served but to serve; not to defend its rights but to defend the rights of men (among which should be included the right to profess the religion the individual conscience chooses); and it should not put its faith in human promises, which are not always disinterested, but in love of God and the power of attraction of the ideal of Jesus.

From the point of view of ethical and religious teaching, the Spanish experience of this period shows that excessive ideological pressure on the young provokes the opposite reaction: there are innumerable cases of families brought up in accordance with the scheme of religious authoritarianism I have described, whose children are now taking an active part in opposition groups radically opposed in every way to the ideology their fathers tried to inculcate in them.

*Translated by Paul Burns*

Kevin Ryan

# Moral Formation: The American Scene

AMERICANS have rediscovered morality recently. Traditionally, a heightened sense of moral purpose has been attributed to the American character. Indeed, this moralistic streak has frequently got Americans into trouble. Much of the incentive to go into south-east Asia and stay so long was motivated by the idea of saving small countries yearning for democracy from the evils of Communism. However, over the last dozen years, America's sense of moral superiority has taken a beating. We have seen our heroes in leaders killed by our own countrymen. We have experienced a convulsive civil rights struggle that has brought an old and vicious streak of racism to the surface. We have had a president thrust from office for deceit compounded by repeated lying. There have been numerous revelations of crime among our top corporate executives. All of these have caused us anguish about the American moral character. One by-product of this general concern for the quality of the American moral character is the apparent heightened interest of the older generation in the moral formation of the young. These last ten years or so have brought a number of, at least, superficial changes in the behaviour of the young. There has been a major increase of teen-age crime and in the use of drugs. The percentage of teen-agers engaging in premarital sex and the percentages afflicted with social diseases has risen sharply. On the other hand, achievement scores in school-related subjects such as reading and writing and mathematics have dropped. The influence of the family is down and the influence of the peer group is up. All of these trends have been making an uneasy older generation even more distressed as they view the behaviour and life styles of the young.

Catholic Americans have had an added dimension to this concern about morality and values. As a result of changes brought about by Vatican II, and particularly in reaction to what is seen as the rigidities of *Humanae Vitae,* the traditional moral certitude of Catholics has been substantially eroded. The phenomenon of receiving radically different pastoral advice on issues like the control of birth has deeply confused Catholics. Also, now that the Church has two and three positions on some issues, it has resulted in a real diminution of its teaching authority. 'If they don't know where they stand, why listen at all'.

American Catholics have also experienced the disorientation of a rather rapid attitude-change from their non-Catholic neighbors. Where once there was a rather wide disapproval of contraception, abortion, premarital sex and to some degree, divorce, rather quickly in the last few years American Catholics have found themselves standing alone. They were not only standing alone, but they were standing against much popular opinion in this country. Indeed, there was as much opinion against the stand of Catholics by other Catholics. We became the ones who were promoting overbreeding. We were keeping birth control regulations on the books in various states. We were fighting the woman's right to control her own body. These factors, then, made for a very confused and muddy picture of what once had been clear.

This unease within the nation, and particularly among American Catholics, has brought renewed interest in the moral development or moral formation of the young. At that time when the nation's attention turned to this question, two approaches to moral development were prominent in educational and psychological circles. These two are the *values clarification* approach pioneered by Louis E. Raths and developed and popularized by Sidney Simon, and second, the *cognitive developmental* approach to moral education developed by Lawrence Kohlberg. Both of them are given extensive coverage in the education literature and to some degree in the popular press. Both approaches are beginning to be applied in the home, the church, and the school.

## VALUES CLARIFICATION

The values clarification approach is captured in the term. The aim is to help the child to clarify what he believes and bring to the surface his own understanding of what he values and what he thinks are the important things in his life. The aim here is simply to help the child gain greater self-knowledge. It is believed that the ability to know one's own values will help people act more consistently and confidently on the basis of those values when faced with moral decisions. On the other hand, advocacy of this approach would discourage teaching of a particular set of morals or values. The role of the values clarificationist is simply to help children explore their own values.

Advocates of values clarification believe that people in our society suffer from a lack of clear values. They point to an array of symptoms, particularly among the young, from apathy to flightiness. These they feel are responses to an inability to make choices about what to do and what they want in a world characterized by over-choice. Values clarificationists are fond of quoting psychologist John Gardner, the former US Secretary of Health, Education and Welfare, on the need for each of us to wrest our own values: 'Instead of giving young people the impression that their task is to stand the dreary watch over the ancient values, we should be telling them the grim but bracing truth that it is their task to recreate those values continually in their own time'.

According to the values clarificationists, then, one recreates one's values as a result of 'hammering out a style of life in a certain set of surroundings'. One gains one's sets of values through a definite process, which is built into the strategies employed by values clarification.

It is imperative, however, to understand what values clarificationists mean by the term 'value'. Theirs is a fairly strict and demanding definition. Unless something satisfies seven criteria they have established, it is not considered a value. These criteria are then:

First, to qualify, something has to be chosen freely. A value cannot be forced on someone. There cannot be any coercion involved.

Second, something has to be chosen from alternatives. If there is only one thing that one can do, that really does not qualify. One has to have a free choice, from alternatives.

Third, to qualify, something has to be chosen after thoughtful consideration of the consequences of that alternative. It cannot be impulsive. It cannot be just something that is done quickly on an impulse.

Fourth, the value must be prized and cherished. It has to be something one respects, one holds dear; something about which one is personally happy.

Fifth, a value is something that one is ready to affirm. That one is ready to tell one's friends about. About which one is ready to make a public affirmation. It is not something hidden away.

Sixth, something is of value only if one acts upon it. If it is merely something that exists in the mind, or perhaps that one talks about, but does not demonstrate with one's behavior, then it does not qualify. One has to be ready to put one's time and energy behind it.

And seventh, something is of value if one does it repeatedly. An occasional interest does not qualify as a value. A value is something that one does on a regular basis. When one has free time, one engages in it. It becomes a part of the pattern of one's life.

So, according to this definition of values, we find out our values by looking at how we behave, how we spend our time and energy.

Consistent with this definition of values, advocates of values clarification believe that positive growth and moral formation comes about through helping children choose freely from among alternatives after consideration of alternatives. The children should be helped to make choices about things which make them happy and which they are ready to do in public. And that they be urged to solidify these values through not just words but by repeated actions. To foster this growth, the values clarificationist engages the student in an array of largely verbal activities. These activities are games or probing questions that attempt to get the young to think about what he really believes in and really wants to do with his time and energy. Moral formation, then, is achieved by helping children find out their own values.

An experienced values clarificationist has at his command hundreds of different strategies and procedures. Only a few can be mentioned here. One of the most common and one of the most fundamental is the clarifying question: that is, the question that helps the child clarify the issue or issues more clearly for himself. For instance, if a teenager were to ask a values clarificationist a question like: 'Should I go to school this summer or should I try out for the swimming team?' the values clarificationist would reply, 'Which would you like to do most?' or 'What do you believe are the consequences of each course of action?' or 'Based on your experience, which do you think would be of greatest value to you?'

If a young person comes up and says: 'I am getting a summer job', instead of saying: 'I'm glad to hear it', or something like that, the values clarificationists respond: 'Are you glad about that?' or 'What were your other options'?

Another technique is called rank order. The aim here is to give the child a choice, to make and publicly affirm that choice and on occasion to explain his choice to other children. A question such as, 'Would you rather be rich, good looking, or smart?' is posed. Then the child, or group of children, is asked to decide and publicly state how they would rank those alternatives. Other rank order types of questions are: 'If I gave you $500, what would you do with it: save it, give it to charity, or buy something for yourself?' and: 'Which do you think more money should be spent on: energy research, slum clearance, or a cure for cancer?'

Another technique is called values voting. Here again, the children are given a chance to publicly affirm what they believe in. A values clarificationist asks a group of students: 'How many of you are . . . ?' and then they ask questions. The young person raises his hand if he has an affirmative opinion. He can put his thumbs down if he has a negative opinion. And, as in all of these exercises, they do not have to commit themselves. The following are examples of values voting: 'How many of you think that at this point in your life you are a complete flop or failure?' 'How many of you have ever felt lonely, even in a crowd of people?' 'How many of you are an only child?' 'How many of you have ever had a scary dream?'

A very popular values clarification strategy is called 'Twenty things I love to do'. The purpose is to have the children identify the things that they really enjoy in life. Then they are asked simply to list down twenty things that they would like to do if they had a free choice. They are not required to list exactly twenty, but the idea is to commit on paper things that they like to spend their time doing. After writing for ten or fifteen minutes, the children are asked to look at the list and asked to put some symbols next to the various choices. First of all, they might put a dollar sign next to all of the items that would cost more than $10. To put an 'A' next to all of those that they can do alone. Things that involve people, they put a 'p' next to. Then, they might be asked to put numbers 1 through 5 by their first five choices, with '1' being for the most important.

At this point a number of things can be done. First of all, the children can break up into pairs and talk over their lists. Or, a teacher might have students write a composition of what they learned about themselves as a result of this exercise.

In all of these values clarification activities, there are a number of principles to be honoured. First of all, no one is forced to participate. Second, the information should not be used by the adult in the future to moralize or to point out the strengths or deficiencies in a values decision. Third, and related, the values clarificationist maintains a totally neutral role. In no way does he indicate his own reactions or value preferences. Basic to his approach is his belief that engaging the young in a values clarification process will result in good things happening. As mentioned earlier, values clarification is the current rage in public and religious circles in the United States. Advocates and supporters are generous in their claims. Engaging in values clarification cures apathy, flightiness, drifting, over-conformity, and over-dissenting. On the positive side, it helps children become 'purposeful, proud, enthusiastic and aware of what is worth striving for in life'. Heady claims, indeed. Unfortunately, these claims are totally innocent of any supporting data.

On the other hand, there are a small but growing number of critics who are raising questions about values clarification. The most troubling is: 'Does values clarification promote unthinking moral relativism?'

Discussions are brief. There is little probing into issues raised. There is the possibility of children leaving values clarification exercises with the belief such as: 'Well, my ideas or my decisions are as good as anyone else's. In matters of values or morality, there are no ways of getting at correctness or incorrectness. There are no standards to apply to choices.'

Other questions are raised about the role of peer pressure. When important issues are raised in values clarification sessions, all there is to guide the child are his own thoughts and those he hears from his peers. Often what is left is a popularity-poll approach to issues of value and morality.

These criticisms in no way seem to dampen the ardor of values clarificationists. In a country hungry to deal with issues of value and morality, this way, which takes little training and doesn't require one to take a stand himself, is an easy way to take on important issues but not have to fiercely commit oneself.

### COGNITIVE DEVELOPMENTAL THEORY

In the early part of the century, the Swiss child psychologist, Jean Piaget, developed a theory of learning which has become increasingly influential in psychological and educational circles. Piaget, through careful observation, noticed that children's thought at various ages had distinctive characteristics. The actual way they thought had characteristic structures. These structures are age related and unfold in a very definite sequence, moving from simple concrete thought to more complex abstract thought. Piaget briefly gave attention to the moral thinking of the young and found clearly discernible stages of moral reasoning in children from five to twelve. However, he did not pursue this research for an extended period.

Approximately twenty-five years ago, a young psychologist, Lawrence Kohlberg, took up Piaget's theory and since that time has attempted to extend and test his theory.

Both Piaget and Kohlberg are concerned with the form of moral thinking rather than the morality or immorality of the actual decision. They are concerned with the mental structures that are called into play to deal with the question of right and wrong. Nor does the cognitive developmental approach pay a great deal of attention to moral behavior. This approach concerns itself with the quality of moral thinking.

Kohlberg's research has uncovered what he believes are six distinct levels of moral thinking; that is, once one has gone beyond the prerational stage of childhood. See Table 1 at the end of this chapter.

The cognitive developmental theory suggests first that there are the six distinct stages of moral thinking and that individuals are capable of moving through them. However, not all people get through all stages—far from it. Only about a third of the adult population reaches stage five and only a relative handful appear to reach stage six. Kohlberg, however, sees it as the role of education to aid people to reach the highest possible level of moral thinking.

One of the possible aspects of this theory is that there would appear to be a *telos,* a dynamic force, that leads us to ever higher levels of moral thinking. Further, certain kinds of educational environment or activities can stimulate growth toward higher levels. For a number of years, Lawrence Kohlberg has been concerned with finding applications for his cognitive developmental theory in public education. Through research, he has been convinced that allowing children to deal with human dilemmas helps them to reach higher levels. For instance, he might suggest the following dilemma to be discussed by high school students:

> You are downtown with a friend, if you are a girl, it's a girl, and if you are a boy, it's a boy. You go to a large department store. You go to the sweater department and while you are there, your friend takes a sweater off the counter and goes into the dressing room. After a few minutes, your friend comes out and she (or he) has the sweater on, but has it on under her coat. Your friend looks at you and motions with her head that she is going out the store door. You don't know what she is doing at first, but then you realize that she is leaving and that she is taking the sweater with her. Startled, you start towards the door, but after two or three steps, someone grabs you and says: 'I have you at least. Your friend got away, but you have not. You're coming down to the manager's office', and he and the manager say the following to you: 'You had better tell us the name of your friend, because you are in big trouble.' What would you do under these circumstances? What do you think would be the *right thing* to do?

At that point students are asked to think about the dilemma and, possibly after clarifying some points, they should decide on a course of action. Then students are grouped together according to what decision they made and told to try to come up with the best reasons why their decision represented the correct thing to do. Then students are asked to exchange the best reasons for their course of action with the aim of convincing those with opposite views. They are free to change sides in this discussion based on what at any one time they think is the correct thing to do.

Kohlberg's research and that of his colleagues suggest that having students discussing dilemmas in this manner will provide substantial and lasting growth in terms of his stages.

Not all discussion or argumentation is conducive to growth. Kohlberg has discovered that presenting people with moral reasoning at a level more than one stage above them has no effect on their stage development. This may account for the apparent low level of success of much of the moral preaching and teaching that has gone on in churches and schools over the centuries. If a teacher is presenting the reasons why someone should behave in a certain fashion in the principled terms of stage five, a young person at stage three may hear and even understand the meaning of the words, but they will not hold together as a compelling moral reason. In effect, he hears the words but does not understand the music.

Another most positive aspect of this theory is that individuals are attracted to moral reasoning at the stage higher than their current stage, but find moral reasoning at a stage lower unsophisticated and uncompelling. In effect, there is an actual attraction to higher levels of moral thinking. Therefore, Kohlberg is confident in promoting moral discussions, particularly when three conditions are present: first, exposure to the next higher stage of reasoning possible; second, as exposure to situations posing problems as contradiction to the child's current moral structure, leading to dissatisfaction with his current level; third, there is an atmosphere of open dialect and exchange in which conflicting moral views are compared.

Although Kohlberg's theory is primarily concerned with moral reasoning, recently he has become interested in moral action. He and others have established what are called "just community schools," usually high schools or sub-groups within high schools. The aim here is to establish an institutional environment where the justice structure stimulates moral growth rather than retards it. Most 'just community schools' are governed by participatory democracy in which the students are given extensive opportunities to grapple with the moral problems involved in the running of the school. The students, with teachers and administrators, must decide on the daily issues of fairness and morality that are raised in school—issues such as stealing, disruptions, grading and the use of drugs. One method used to insure that higher stage thinking is promoted is to precede all school meetings with small group moral discussions. Such an approach is seen as a means of promoting high level moral thinking in the actual school decision making.

These cognitive developmental applications to school are still in the very early stage. Also, they are not nearly as widely known or practised as the values clarification activities mentioned above. Nevertheless, a good deal of interest and controversy has been aroused by this approach to moral education. Some discount Kohlberg's theory, going to the very heart of his six stages of development. They call into question the empirical evidence Kohlberg cites for the existence of these stages. Others question the viability of this approach on the grounds that it is too sophisticated for the average teacher or parent. They cite the fact that if only a third of the adults are at stage five, there are many parents and teachers, who are at lower levels and their capacity to interpret this material is doubtful at best.

TWO LIMITATIONS

To this writer, there are two major deficiencies in these two approaches toward the moral education of the young. And these deficiencies severely restrict their value. First, is the lack of concern for the actual content of a moral decision; and second, is the lack of concern for moral behaviour:

## *Moral Thought*

Both the values clarification strategies and the dilemma based curriculum of the cognitive developmentalist deal with intellectual operations, but not with the content or product of thought. Values clarificationists want the child to discover and own his own values and make decisions based upon his values. On the other hand, Lawrence Kohlberg is concerned with long-term growth resulting from the cognitive clash of opposing views. In terms of the dilemma of the teenagers in the department store appearing above, the values clarificationists would feel that their work had been done well if the teenager left behind had, after careful reflection and weighing of the alternatives, turned in his friend to the authorities. To Kohlberg, the outcome of the teenage dilemma is of little concern. It is the form of his thinking, its cognitive complexity, rather than the actual decision with which he is concerned. It should be acknowledged, however, that both the values clarificationists and the cognitive developmentalists aim at some long term positive results which they believe will occur if their particular strategies are followed. In the meantime, they are not concerned with the day-to-day moral decisions made by the young. This, I believe, is a glaring weakness and disqualifies both approaches for any major role in dictating policies for moral education. Those who follow these approaches exclusively ignore a whole tradition in western thought. That is, the application of reasoned issues of right and wrong. They would not attempt to teach the young the principles of the moral life, such as respect for others' property, the need for fairness and the like. These approaches do not attempt to teach skills of moral thinking, such as consistency, causal and noncausal relationships, and how to use inference correctly. Efforts to directly educate the young through stories, examples and the application of rational skills to all situations are ignored.

Such a lack of foundation in a moral education programme seems tragic. It is casting aside an intellectual heritage for some untested and surely incomplete method of helping the young toward moral development. It also seems strikingly anti-intellectual. At times when the hard eye of reasoned analysis is in focus on every other corner of human existence, to leave the domain of moral values and moral action out-of-bounds to rational analysis seems questionable. If, as some say, we're living off the moral sensibilities forged in past eras and that the present self-centered moral motif is wearing thin, then we need intellectual skills to reclaim the unifying moral principles on which society is dependent.

## Moral Action

The second major criticism of these two popular approaches is that they ignore behavior. Mental practice at clarifying one's values or working on dilemmas does not guarantee, or even provide much confidence, that a child will learn to do good and avoid evil. I believe most people know from their own experience that, first, moral behavior does not just happen. It is an outcome of moral education. To clarify one's values for oneself or to solve dilemmas or even to develop a fine sense of justice would be of little value if one does not behave in a moral manner. What are the value of intellectual achievements in the moral domain, if one continues to interfere with the rights of one's neighbour or knowingly causes pain to those around him. Second, we know we can and we must teach the young how to behave. We know that children must be taught directly, and often forcefully, not to hurt other children. We know that we must clarify, often repeatedly, for the young what their values ought to be and how they should behave. We need to present the young with models of men and women behaving well. We need to do this through stories and accounts of virtuous behavior, but also by our own behavior as parents and teachers.

In the current discussion of moral education in the United States, Aristotle's view of how men become virtuous has all but been lost. Aristotle believed that a man became brave by doing brave acts, that a man became kind by engaging in acts of kindness. In effect, one becomes moral by behaving in moral ways. This approach has been severely eroded recently. Perhaps, it is because many are unsure what is virtuous. Is it really wise to be concerned about and to respect one's fellow man? Is it smart to give to others when there is no clear assurance that the gift will be responded to? We have also lowered our expectations of such things as service. As a result, children are given relatively few opportunities in schools and in our communities to be of service to one another, to share one's gifts or wealth and particularly to give of one's time and energy. On the whole, however, little altruistic behavior is expected of many modern children and one suspects little is being developed. Also, if we are not giving our children opportunities to behave in moral ways, then we should not be surprised when they do not know how to behave as morally independent people.

One interesting exception to this lack is a programme recently adopted by many Jesuit high schools in this country:

> Each high school student must perform one hundred hours of service from a wide variety of choice before graduation. Service to others is part of the curriculum and a condition of receiving a diploma.

## CONCLUSION

In summary, the current dialogue about moral education in the United States is dominated by two new and untested approaches. Perhaps because they have come after a period of moral conflict and confusion, they are each being treated as the only way to approach the moral education of the young. While confident that the passage of time will put these approaches into better perspective, one question does persist. Why have the religious educators in our Catholic schools and universities become so quickly and totally enamoured of these approaches? Why have they de-emphasized traditional intellectual training, the teaching about standards of right and wrong and the opportunity to serve, for such meagre fare as values clarification and cognitive developmental moral education?

### TABLE 1. DEFINITION OF MORAL STAGES

*1. Preconventional level*

At this level, the child is responsive to cultural rules and labels of good and bad, right or wrong, but interprets these labels either in terms of the physical or the hedonistic consequences of action (punishment, reward, exchange of favors) or in terms of the physical power of those who enunciate the rules and labels. The level is divided into the following two stages:

Stage 1: *The punishment-and-obedience orientation*. The physical consequences of action determine its goodness or badness, regardless of the human
meaning or value of these consequences. Avoidance of punishment and un-
questioning deference to power are valued in their own right, not in terms of
respect for an underlying moral order supported by punishment and authority
(the latter being Stage 4).

Stage 2: *The instrumental-relativist orientation*. Right action consists of that
which instrumentally satisfies one's own needs and occasionally the needs of
others. Human relations are viewed in terms like those of the marketplace.
Elements of fairness, of reciprocity, and of equal sharing are present, but they
are always interpreted in a physical, pragmatic way. Reciprocity is a matter of
'you scratch my back and I'll scratch yours', not of loyalty, gratitude, or
justice.

## 2. Conventional level

At this level, maintaining the expectations of the individual's family, group,
or nation is perceived as valuable in its own right, regardless of immediate and
obvious consequences. The attitude is not only one of *conformity* to personal
expectations and social order, but of loyalty to it, of actively *maintaining,*
supporting, and justifying the order, and of identifying with the persons or
group involved in it. At this level, there are the following two stages:

Stage 3: *The interpersonal concordance or "good boy—nice girl" orientation.*
Good behavior is that which pleases or helps others and is approved by them.
There is much conformity to stereotypical images of what is majority or "natural" behavior. Behavior is frequently judged by intention—"he means well"
becomes important for the first time. One earns approval by being 'nice'.

Stage 4: *The 'law and order' orientation*. There is orientation toward authority, fixed rules, and the maintenance of the social order. Right behavior consists of doing one's duty, showing respect for authority, and maintaining the
given social order for its own sake.

## 3. Postconventional, autonomous, or principled level

At this level, there is a clear effort to define moral values and principles that
have validity and application apart from the authority of the groups or persons
holding these principles and apart from the individual's own identification with
these groups. This level also has two stages:

Stage 5: *The social-contract, legalistic orientation,* generally with utilitarian
overtones. Right action tends to be defined in terms of general individual rights
and standards which have been critically examined and agreed upon by the
whole society. There is a clear awareness of the relativism of personal values
and opinions and a corresponding emphasis upon procedural rules for reaching
consensus. Aside from what is constitutionally and democratically agreed
upon, the right is a matter of personal 'values' and 'opinion'. The result is an
emphasis upon the 'legal point of view', but with an emphasis upon the possibility of changing law in terms of rational considerations of social utility (rather

than freezing it in terms of Stage 4 'law and order'). Outside the legal realm, free agreement and contract is the binding element of obligation. This is the 'official' morality of the American government and constitution.

Stage 6: *The universal-ethical-principle orientation.* Right is defined by the decision of conscience in accord with self-chosen *ethical principles* appealing to logical comprehensiveness, universality, and consistency. These principles are abstract and ethical (the Golden Rule, the categorical imperative); they are not concrete moral rules like the Ten Commandments. At heart, these are universal principles of *justice,* of the *reciprocity* and *equality* of human *rights,* and of respect for the dignity of human beings as *individual persons* ('From Is to Ought', pp. 164–5).

Reprinted from *The Journal of Philosophy,* 25 October 1973

# Contributors

ALFONS AUER was born in Schöneberg, Germany, in 1915. He is Professor of Theological Ethics in Tübingen and has published a number of works on the history of piety, morality and ethics.

MIGUEL BENZO was born in Madrid in 1922. Since 1960 he has been Professor of Religion at the Madrid Centre of University Studies. He is also Professor of Theological Anthropology at the Madrid Seminary and holds other major teaching posts. He has published on anthropology, the sacraments, and ethics.

PIERRE CAMELOT was born in Lille in 1901. He is Professor of Classical Philology at the Lille Catholic Faculties. He has made a major contribution to the charismatic renewal. He has published many historical and spiritual studies, and patristic and conciliar essays.

HELMUT JUROS was born in Silesia in 1933. He is Professor of Moral Theology at the Catholic Theological Academy in Warsaw. He has published a study of G. E. Moore's ethical system and other important essays on ethics and philosophical theology.

HENRI DE LAVALETTE is Professor of Theology at the Catholic Institute in Paris and a member of the editorial committee of *Recherches de Science Religieuse* where he is in charge of the standard bulletins on fundamental theology and political theology.

ROLAND MURPHY was born in Chicago in 1917. He is an American Carmelite and a member of the Editorial Board of *Concilium*. He is Professor of Old Testament studies at Duke University Divinity School in Durham, U.S.A., and the author of several works on the Old Testament.

JOHANNES NEUMANN was born in Königsberg in 1929 and is Professor of Canon Law at Tübingen University. He has published major works on confirmation, marriage law, and German canon law and ecclesiology.

JACQUES POHIER was born in France in 1926. He was a Professor in the Saulchoir Faculties. Among his publications are leading works on psychology, psychoanalysis and theology.

NORBERT RIGALI, S. J., studied at Innsbruck and Munich and wrote a doctoral thesis on Karl Jaspers' existentialism. He has published a number of articles on moral theology and is currently Professor of Theology and Chairperson of the Department of Religious Studies at the University of San Diego.

KEVIN RYAN is Associate Dean for Programme Development and Professor of Curriculum and Foundations in the College of Education at Ohio State University. He has taught on the education courses of Stanford and Harvard universities. He has written seven books and many articles regarding morals and particularly moral education.

ANTOINE VERGOTE was born in 1921 in Kortrijk. He is a leading expert in religious psychology and teaches at Louvain University in Belgium. He has taken a leading part in international congresses, journals and so on and his book on religious psychology has been translated into a number of languages.